What Are You Waiting For?

Introduction

My Story

You may be asking yourself, "What qualifies this guy to write this book?" What qualifies me is that I've been there. I've been to the bottom and back. I sank to some of the lowest points a human being can go—mentally, physically, spiritually, emotionally, and financially. I was all the way down, as far down as I ever want to go again. Amazingly, though, as far down as I was, I was able to turn things around and climb back from the devastation that my life had become, all by applying the ideas discussed in this book.

Through a chain of events and circumstances, totally caused by my own actions, my life had become a total disaster. I was living in a small, rented room with a shared bathroom in the South Bronx, one of the worst neighborhoods in New York City. I'll never forget the cockroaches. They were so bold they didn't even run when the light was turned on. Instead, they stood there as if to say, "What are you doing in my bathroom?" I was barely able to pay the $45-a-week rent. What little money I was earning from day jobs was going to support my drinking habit. I had no friends left because, as a result of my excesses, I had become impossible to be around.

My health was failing rapidly due to my lifestyle and poor eating habits.

I had, as they say, reached the bottom. I had done it all. Sold my belongings, slept in cars, gone without food for days at a time, been evicted, and all the other indignities that are part and parcel of that lifestyle. About the only thing I did not do was panhandle or steal.

I remember one spring evening walking down Broadway in New York City and instead of looking at the bright lights and majestic skyline, I was looking at the ground—trying to find a nickel so I would have enough money to buy a pack of cigarettes. There were days when I would walk 20 blocks uptown to 96th Street where I could buy loose cigarettes for ten cents each. Talk about walking a mile for a Camel!

THE TURNING POINT

I finally reached my bottom. I had fallen as low as I could stand. I reached that point where something inside of me said, "This has to change—now!" I was fortunate that I had parents who were willing to take me in and give me one more chance. If it were not for them, I would have wound up living in Central Park or worse.

I'm not sure exactly what the turning point was. I know I had taken all the emotional pain I could stand and even thought about taking my own life. My once promising life had become a disaster. I had squandered the talents and gifts I was born with, and I made a decision that I had to your family deserves the best life possible. Most of all, do it now! *What are you waiting for? It's YOUR life!*

MAKING THE MOST OF THIS BOOK

If you don't already have a journal, it would be a great idea to get one. It has been said that a life worth living is worth recording. Journals don't need to be elaborate. A simple spiral notebook works just fine. It's like keeping a diary—a place where you can record your thoughts, observations, and feelings, a place to write your dreams, your goals, and your plans. Many people write in their journals every day, although that's not necessary.

One of the great things about keeping a journal is being able to go back through the years and realize how far I've come. I've been writing in a journal for almost ten years now, and I love periodically reading what I wrote from years past. It's inspiring to see how much I've changed and realize how many of my dreams have come true.

Throughout this book there are exercises. Please do them. Write them in your journal or in the back of this book. As I said earlier, these principles work, but only if you use them.

I suggest you read through the entire book. Then go back and invest some time doing the exercises. This is where the real benefit lies. You can read all the books ever written, but if you don't put the ideas into practice, nothing will change. Most people already know what to do to improve their lives. The question is: are you willing to do it?

YOU CAN CHANGE YOUR LIFE FOR THE BETTER

It does not matter where you are starting from or how far down you may have fallen. You *can* have lifelong success. You can turn your life around from wherever you are. I have been at the bottom. I know how it feels. I also know that you can change your circumstances. I have done it, and I have witnessed many others do the same.

The information in this book is not theory. These aren't just a bunch of "nice ideas." They are *proven principles that work*. These ideas have stood the test of time. I have personally used these ideas and techniques in my own life. They were passed on to me by others, and I'm passing them on to you. I have used these ideas to make major changes in my own life. I know they work, and I know that if they worked for me, they'll work for you. I have taught these strategies in seminars and workshops and have seen, firsthand, the results people produced by applying these simple techniques.

IT'S UP TO YOU

If you want to achieve lifelong success, you can; however, *only you can do it*. I cannot change your life. No book ever written can change your life. In the end, it's up to you.

Don't take what is here on blind faith. Work with the ideas, test them, question them. If something here is in conflict with your belief, leave it. Take only what works for you. This is your life. You deserve it to be the best you can make

What Are You Waiting For?

It's YOUR Life!

JIM DONOVAN

Sound Wisdom
167 Walnut Bottom Road
Shippensburg, PA 17257

www.soundwisdom.com
717-530-2122

This book and all other Sound Wisdom books are available at bookstores and distributors worldwide.

Previously published as *This Is Your Life, Not A Dress Rehearsal, Proven Principles For Creating The Life Of Your Dreams* by Bovan Publishing Group.

Previous ISBN: 0-9650534-2-3

ISBN 13 TP: 978-1-937879-34-1
ISBN 13 Ebook: 978-1-937879-35-8

For Worldwide Distribution, Printed in the U.S.A.
4 5 6 7 8 9 10 /16 15 14

Contents

it. You deserve to have the life of your dreams. You deserve lifelong success.

READY, SET, SUCCEED!

Fasten your seat belt, for you are about to embark on a ride that can be so incredible, so inspiring, so exciting, so grand, so powerful—and it just keeps getting better and better and better. Enjoy your journey and the experiences life has to offer. Begin now to live the life of your dreams.

What Are You Waiting For?

Do it now! Whatever it is you have been putting off, do it. *It's your life,* it's not a dress rehearsal. What is it you have always wanted to do but for some unknown reason never quite get around to doing? I'm referring to those usually minor desires, not major goals like "get married" or "start a business."

For me it has been things like swim with dolphins and ride in a glider plane. These were not major accomplishments; but still, for some reason, I had been putting them off for years. Why? Why is it we have a tendency to treat our desires as though we will live forever?

In truth, our time here on this earth is but a brief moment. If we compare our perhaps 100 years here to the age of this planet we call home, we are only here for a blink in time.

What are you putting off? What are some of the things you have always wanted to experience but are postponing because you think you have all the time in the world?

Read the obituaries in today's newspaper and realize that everyone whose name is listed there thought they had another day. It's not my intent to offend you, but I do want to shock you into the realization that *this is it!* It's your life.

YOUR LIFE IS PRECIOUS

Don't treat your life lightly. Live now! Have you always wanted to sky dive? Visit the Great Pyramids? Swim with dolphins? See Niagara Falls? Whatever it is you have always wanted to do but have been putting off, decide now to do it. Make a plan. Determine what you will need to do to prepare. Find out the costs involved. Take action.

When I started writing this book I had still not experienced flying in a glider plane, even though it was something I really wanted to do. There were no logical reasons why I had not done it. I simply kept putting it off. It was always in my "someday I'll" file.

Someday is now! I'm pleased to say that now, as I'm putting the finishing touches on this book, I have experienced the thrill of sailing through the sky in total silence. I decided to take my own advice and make "someday" now. It was great! Doing it was simple enough. All I needed to do was take action.

In your journal or below, answer the following questions:

• What is it you have always wanted to do?

• What preparations will you need to make?

• What is your target date to complete this?

Okay, now think seriously about the following questions:

• Whose life are you living?

• Are you living *your* dream or someone else's dream?

• How much of your life is being decided by someone else?

• Are you in a profession you dislike because it's expected of you?

• Do you engage in activities you would rather skip, simply because it's part of your "role" as a father or mother, daughter or son, spouse or friend? What about you? Doesn't your opinion count?

It's not only reasonable, but mentally healthy for you to direct your own life. If you find yourself in a profession you don't especially like, try asking yourself the following question: if I were starting over in my career, what would I choose to do?

After some people retire, they begin a second career. This time, they do what they love and many times become highly successful.

FAMOUS THE SECOND TIME AROUND

Did you know that Carroll O'Connor, the actor who created the role of Archie Bunker in the television show "All in the Family" and later played the burly police chief in "In the Heat of the Night," was a high school teacher until he was in his 40s? While teaching is surely a noble profession, his greatest gifts were clearly to come from his acting talents. Fortunately for the millions of viewers entertained by his talents, he followed his bliss and became an actor.

Another example of a successful second career is comedienne Phyllis Diller. She was a cleaning lady until she was 37 years of age. Incidentally, she was inspired to ignite her unused potential by reading a self-help book, *The Magic of Believing,* by Claude Bristol. Interestingly enough, Liberace, the great pianist, attributed the strategies in this same book to his huge success and enormous wealth.

TAKE CHARGE OF YOUR LIFE

You owe it to yourself to run your own life. I'm not suggesting that you go out and change everything overnight; however, you can begin to direct your life where you would like it to go.

For example, if you have always wanted to be an actress or actor but have financial responsibilities that require you to work a "real job," you could satisfy your need to act by joining a local theater group. Many community theater performers work happily at a nine-to-five job Monday through Friday, knowing they have an outlet for their creative selves on the weekend.

If all of your time is being taken up in the role of wife and mother, set aside time for yourself—time to pursue your other dreams. You could arrange for your spouse, parent, or either change or die. Frankly, at that point in my life, it did not really matter to me which it was.

While I was living in a room in my parents' apartment, I prayed; actually, I begged God to do something with me. Not long after that painful time, I found the help I needed, and I was on a path to recovery. Before that time, I thought my life was over. I now know this time was just the beginning.

I received a lot of help and support during my darkest hours. If you are struggling with a serious problem like addiction, get professional help. Don't try to go it alone. Call a support program, your doctor, minister, priest, rabbi, therapist, or someone who is qualified to help in these matters. This is a life-and-death situation and should not be taken lightly.

I'm not writing this to gain your sympathy or to impress you with my struggle. I'm sharing my story so you can realize that no matter how far down you may have fallen, there is hope.

Most of the people who will read this book have not, hopefully, gone as far down as I did. Most have jobs, houses, and families; however, I know they—you—have your challenges too. While your personal situation may not be as dramatic as my experience, it's no less important.

Perhaps you are experiencing financial difficulties. Maybe you're in a dead-end job with no future or you're worried about downsizing (that's a modern word for being fired for no apparent reason). Your health may be less than ideal. Perhaps your relationship with your family could use improvement.

Maybe everything is great in your life and you merely want it to be the best it can be. We all want to grow and expand our horizons. There is always more to give and do and have and become. It's human nature to want to experience the best life has to offer.

This is a simple book. I share simple, practical strategies and techniques that anyone can use. By applying the principles in this book, you can go from wherever you are in your life at this moment, to living a life that is truly the life of your dreams.

TODAY

Today, many years later, I sometimes pinch myself when I look at the wonderful life I'm living. I'm now doing work I love and am having a positive effect on people's lives. I'm totally committed to my work. And I look forward to each new day with excitement and enthusiasm, anxious to begin it.

I'm happily married to a wonderful and supportive woman, Georgia, and have a loving family, dear friends, and live in a dream home with every luxury I could want, nestled in the woods in beautiful Bucks County, Pennsylvania.

I have more than I ever imagined. But most of all, I'm at peace. My life has a purpose, as does yours. We are all here to make a contribution that is uniquely ours. We all have our parts to play in this drama of life.

Please don't just read this book—use it! Apply it. Take from it what you need to make your life everything it can be. Do it now because you deserve it. Do it now because close friend to take care of your children a few hours each week while you take care of your own needs.

Taking care of yourself is not selfish. Give yourself permission to treat yourself as someone special. Begin to set aside time to do some of the things you want to do for yourself. You will become a more relaxed and contented person, which will in turn make you a more agreeable and cheerful person with those around you. Everyone wins!

If you are in a job you strongly dislike, start devising a plan that will allow you to make a change. Perhaps you need to seek retraining in another profession. I know of several nurses who, when they realized they were spending more time filling out paperwork than caring for patients, began new careers as massage therapists. This gave them the satisfaction of working directly with people.

What are you waiting for?

Chapter 1

Acceptance and Attitude

The last of the human freedoms is to choose one's
attitude in any given set of circumstances.
–Viktor Frankl

Years ago when I lived in New York City and actually had a job, I took the subway to work. Usually there were hundreds of people on the platform waiting for the train. Sometimes the trains were late for one reason or another, and I used to watch as a few of the commuters became anxious and stressed, trying to "make" the train come.

We've all seen this type of person. I'll call him "Hyper Harry." Hyper Harry would begin pacing up and down the platform, looking at his watch, then leaning over and looking down the track to see if the train was coming. He would continue this ritual of pacing, looking, and leaning as if doing this ritual would somehow cause the train to arrive. Meanwhile, his blood pressure was rising, and I could see the veins in his neck popping. I noticed that no matter how fast Harry paced, the train did not come any sooner. All of his pacing and anxiety had no affect whatsoever on the train. All it did was stress him out. Clearly this was a situation Harry couldn't change. He would have been happier and more at peace if he had simply accepted his powerlessness in the situation.

The moral of the story is that while we cannot change many situations, we can always change how we view them and how they affect us.

Like Hyper Harry, do you allow a situation that is out of your control to cause you emotional turmoil? Think about it the next time you start pacing and your veins start popping.

ACCEPTANCE AND DENIAL

Acceptance is the first key to lifelong success. Acceptance means accepting ourselves, our conditions, and the world around us as it is, not how we wish it to be. It means getting out of denial and getting honest with ourselves. It means analyzing a situation and accepting that which we cannot control or change. It means having the courage to change those things that are in our power to change. It means being wise enough to know the difference between the two.

When I talk about denial, I'm not talking about the river in Africa, I'm talking about people being 50 pounds overweight and rationalizing it by telling themselves they have "big bones." Are their bones really big, or are they simply overweight from eating too much and not exercising?

Accept yourself as you are right now—good or bad. Be honest with yourself and acknowledge where you are. I'm not suggesting that you should not consider reducing your weight to a more healthy number. I'm simply suggesting that you must first accept and acknowledge your present condition.

People who have overcome addictions to alcohol, drugs, food, or gambling have first had to admit and accept their problem. This acceptance demonstrates your willingness to "own" the problem which in turn gives you the power to change it.

Affirm that you have created your current situation, either consciously or unconsciously, take responsibility for it, and become willing to change. The more you can accept the reality of *what is* instead of how you wish things were, the closer you are to creating a happy and successful life.

ACCEPT YOURSELF

Too many of us have bought into negative self-images. The major social problems in our society—drug addiction, alcoholism, crime, teenage gangs, divorce, and most others—begin with a poor self-image and low self-esteem. Most criminals have low self-esteem. All you need to do to confirm this is visit a prison and talk to the inmates. The first thing you will notice is that they continually look down at the floor when speaking to you. This is a dead giveaway of a low self-image.

During one of my workshops, a woman remarked how she did not like going to events and meeting new people because, as she put it, "Then they will know how dumb I am." The truth of the matter is that she is a very intelligent person but has developed a negative self-image and allowed it to limit her experience.

Louise Hay, the bestselling author, suggests we work with the affirmation, "I approve of myself." I urge you to try this for yourself, especially if you have a low self-image. If you want to get a quick read on your present level of self-esteem, stand in front of a mirror and say aloud, "I approve of myself." Don't be surprised if it makes you uncomfortable, even scared. I have seen people burst into tears doing this exercise. However, if you continue to do this, over time, you will begin to experience changes in how you feel about yourself and in your life in general. Louise suggests you recite, write, and sing these words 300-400 times a day!

Practice receiving a compliment with a simple "Thank you" instead of brushing it off by saying, "It's no big deal." You deserve compliments. You deserve love. You deserve happiness.

It's useful to keep in mind that while you will never be perfect, you can become a perfect you. Personally, I have always liked the concept that my life is a work of art in progress. Like an artist working on a painting, I can work to improve different areas of my life. I'm constantly changing, growing, and evolving—refining a little at a time. Of course it will never be fully completed. Life is about continually changing and growing for the better.

By identifying the areas of your life you want to change, you are on your way to building lifelong success. Later we will develop definite plans for making changes, but for now, simply identify what it is you want to change.

To become clearer about the changes you want to make, complete the following exercise.

Exercise – Acceptance

On a sheet of paper, in your journal, or on the blank pages in the back of this book, draw six boxes large enough to write several lines. Label them with the six major areas of your life:

• Family/social

• Business/career

• Health/fitness

• Spiritual/emotional

• Finances/wealth

• Mental/education

For each area, ask yourself what it is you would like to change or improve. For example, if you are overweight and have health challenges, write that in the box marked "Health/Fitness." If your income is not what you would like it to be, write "increase income" in the "Finances" box.

You will, most likely, have something in each of the boxes. That's okay. Remember, we are all in a constant state of evolving.

ATTITUDE

Another key to lifelong success is *attitude*. Your attitude affects everything in your life. How's your attitude? Are you one of those people who is always blaming outside forces for your problems? Do you walk around in a negative state of mind most of the time? I think not. People like that would never have opened this book in the first place.

However positive you may be most of the time, there will be days when you just feel negative. While this may be fine for a brief period, prolonging a negative attitude has disastrous consequences. A negative attitude robs your initiative and destroys your discipline.

The "so what" or "who cares" attitude stops you from taking the actions that will help you build the kind of life you want to have for yourself and your family.

WHAT HAPPENS?

Here's how a negative attitude robs us of our potential for good. At one of the low points in my life, I had developed a "who cares, what's the use" attitude. I felt that I was stuck where I was because of circumstances outside my control and blamed the world for my conditions. I figured I was at the bottom, so why even care? The problem is, as I learned through a lot of emotional pain, there are always lower bottoms to which I could sink. As my attitude continued to be negative and blaming, my situation worsened.

Only when I was willing to take responsibility for my life, stop blaming, and look for what little good remained, was I able to begin to turn around my situation.

A negative attitude keeps us from advancing our lives by robbing us of the self-discipline we need to improve our conditions. If you take a "what's the use" approach to your circumstances, they will only get worse. It's imperative that you turn a negative attitude around and learn to become a positive person. Use the principles, techniques, and ideas in this book to assist you.

GRATITUDE

The fastest and easiest way I know to change from a negative to a positive attitude is to develop an attitude of gratitude. You may even want to keep a gratitude journal, a place where you can build a list of the things you are grateful for in your life.

It's impossible to have gratitude and be in self-pity at the same time; most negative attitudes are rooted in self-pitying, "poor me" self-talk. You can quickly change a negative attitude to a positive one by becoming grateful.

The simplest way I know to do this is to ask a question like, "What am I grateful for today?" Then write down whatever comes to mind. It may be all of the blessings you have like good health, a clear mind, a loving family, satisfying work, a comfortable home, friends, pets, and so on.

Make a daily habit of counting your blessings and list what you are grateful for in your life. Doing this first thing in the morning will help you feel better immediately and begin your day on a positive note.

On days when you are feeling down, take out your "gratitude journal" and reread it. Doing this simple exercise will make you feel better almost immediately.

ACTION

While we will discuss action in more detail later in this book, I wanted to touch on it here because this one simple distinction can have a major impact in your life.

Too many of us spend our lives fence sitting, trying to decide what to do in any given situation. One of the chief characteristics of virtually all highly successful people is that they make decisions quickly and rarely, if ever, change them.

Unsuccessful people, on the other hand, take a long time deciding what to do and change their minds at the drop of a hat.

When you are faced with making a decision, after carefully weighing the facts, make your choice and act on it immediately. In almost any situation, *doing something* is usually better than sitting still and waiting for something to happen.

There have been times in my business life when I didn't know what to do next—times when I was scared and confused. If you own a business, you can probably identify with this situation. What I found was that if I took action—went out and met people, made a call, wrote a letter—the situation would begin to change for the better. Taking action puts us in what is known as the "path of probability." You're a lot better off doing something than just sitting around waiting for something to happen.

Our tendency, especially in stressful situations, is to become like the ostrich and put our heads in the sand—or under the blankets as the case may be. Gripped by fear, we do nothing. The problem is that doing nothing produces the same result—nothing!

Taking action will always produce a result. If you are unsure about what to do, especially in your business, *do something*. Do whatever comes to mind first. As you begin taking action, keep going and the right action will become clear to you.

Edgar Cayce said, "Trust in the Divine, apply what you know, and the next step will be given."

Immediate Action Exercise

Write in your journal any situations or challenges you are facing. Next to each one, write one simple action you can take immediately to help resolve it. For example:

Challenge 1: *My client base isn't as large as it could be.*

Action: *Draft a letter to potential clients.*

Challenge 2:

Action:

Challenge 3:

Action:

Once you've accepted your situation, shifted your attitude, and decided to act, the next step on your way to creating the life of your dreams is believing. Believe that you can do something about your situation.

Whatever it is you want to change, it's critical for you to develop the belief that you can change it. If you feel stuck and think you are a victim of circumstances, you first need to change your belief to one of possibility and power.

One reason to identify the changes you want to make and accept and "own" everything in your life is so you gain the power to change them.

Chapter 2

Beliefs

What would you attempt to do if you knew you could not fail? –Dr. Robert Schuller

Henry Ford said, "Whether you believe you can, or you believe you can't, you're right." The quality of your life, your actions, and your accomplishments are all determined by your beliefs. This is a powerful and challenging statement; however, it's one that you'll realize is true once you have examined the concept of beliefs.

WHY ELEPHANTS DON'T RUN

A number of years ago I had the rather unique experience of visiting backstage when the Ringling Brothers Barnum and Bailey Circus was performing in Madison Square Garden in New York. To say the least, it was a fascinating experience. I walked around looking at the lions, tigers, giraffes, and all the other circus animals. As I was passing the elephants, I suddenly stopped, confused by the fact that these huge creatures were being held by only a small rope tied to their front leg. No chains, no cages. It was obvious that the elephants could at any time break away from their bonds, but for some reason they did not. I saw a trainer nearby and asked why these beautiful, magnificent animals made no attempt to get away.

"Well," he said, "when they are very young and much smaller, we use the same size rope to tie them and, at that age, it's enough to hold them. As they grow up, they are conditioned to believe they cannot break away. They believe the rope can still hold them, so they never try to break free."

I was amazed. These animals could at any time break free from their bonds, but because they believed they couldn't, they were stuck right where they were. I am not in any way endorsing this horrible treatment of animals. On the contrary. Only when we treat all living things as having value, will we truly value ourselves.

Like the elephants, how many of us go through life hanging on to a belief that we cannot do something simply because we failed at it once before? How many of us are being held back by old, outdated beliefs that no longer serve us? How many of us have avoided trying something new because of a limiting belief? Worse, how many of us are being held back by someone else's limiting beliefs?

BELIEFS AREN'T FACTS

Just because someone believes something cannot be done (even by a large group of people) does not make it true. Be careful not to confuse beliefs with facts. People used to believe a person couldn't run a mile in less than four minutes—until a man named Roger Banister did it and proved them wrong. Today, high school students break the four-minute mile. At one time, everyone believed the world was flat. Did that make it so? Of course not. But until a young man named Christopher Columbus came along, it was a widely held belief. Until Louis Pasteur, most of society didn't believe in germs and bacteria, largely because they couldn't see them.

One word of caution here, be careful of global beliefs and social proof. That's when enough people agree on something that it is assumed to be fact. People told Wilbur and Orville Wright that they were crazy—humans were not meant to fly. Right! And automobiles will never replace horse-drawn carriages.

At this point you may be asking, "What does all this have to do with me and my lifelong success?" Well, it has everything to do with you and your lifelong success. The effort that you expend and the results that you achieve are directly related to your beliefs. In the notable words of Napoleon Hill, author of *Think and Grow Rich,* "Whatever you can conceive and believe, you can achieve."

BEWARE OF LIMITING BELIEFS

If you own a business and you hold a limiting belief that you aren't very good in sales (this is a common belief held by many non-sales professionals), the effort you expend won't tap your true potential, and you will produce a less-than-desirable result.

Let's look at this idea more closely. Most people would agree that human potential is essentially unlimited. If so, then why don't we see this in our own lives? The problem and the reason most people aren't demonstrating their limitless potential is that their actions are tempered by their limiting beliefs. Because of a limiting belief, we tap only a small portion of our potential, which in turn causes us to take limited action resulting in a limited outcome.

In the case of your sales efforts, if you hold the belief that you aren't a good sales person, your effort will be half-hearted. You may only make a few sales calls, and your results will be poor. You compound the problem by using the poor result as reinforcement for your limiting belief. You may say, and believe, something like, "See, I told you I can't sell this stuff."

On the other hand, if you develop a belief that says, "I'm a great sales person," you will tap more of your potential, use more of your inherent creativity, and take more action. Your belief coupled with action will produce a greater result. Successful people assume success to be the natural outcome of their efforts.

Wayne Dyer wrote a book titled *Transformation, You'll See It When You Believe It*. Dyer's simple yet powerful philosophy is that when you begin to believe in your success, you'll see the result in your life. When you begin to believe in your ability to reach your goals, you'll see your beliefs manifest on a physical plane.

CHALLENGING YOUR BELIEFS

In starting or managing a business, for example, we are cautioned not to take risks, usually by well-intentioned friends and family. Have you perhaps heard, "You can't do that!" These are the dream stealers who, due to their own limiting beliefs, will attempt to discourage you from living your dreams. You must ignore them at all cost! I'm not suggesting that you should not seek advice from qualified individuals and mentors, but I am suggesting that you avoid like the plague being swayed by the limiting beliefs of others, especially people who don't have their own businesses.

Challenge your own limiting beliefs by questioning them. If you begin to question a belief, you automatically weaken it. The more you question your limiting beliefs, the more they are weakened. It's like kicking the legs out from under a stool. Once you weaken one leg, the stool loses its balance and falls.

WE ALL SELL

Think back to a time when you "sold" someone on yourself. We are selling all the time. You have to sell your ideas to your spouse, your children, your employees—even your banker. Maybe as a child you sold Girl Scout cookies or magazine subscriptions to raise money for your school team. Even though it was for your school, that was selling too!

Once you realize you are, in fact, a capable salesperson, you have weakened that old belief and begin to replace it with a new, empowering one. Look for references to support the new beliefs you want to cultivate. As in the example of the stool, you want to reinforce your beliefs by adding more and more "legs" to them. Find people who have accomplished what you want to accomplish, discover what they did, and model their behavior.

Remember back to times in your past when you were successful and use that experience to propel yourself forward. If your challenge is in sales, read sales books and listen to tapes or attend sales seminars. Strengthen your sales "legs" so that you strengthen your belief. Whatever you do, don't be undermined by limiting beliefs.

ACT AS IF

There is a technique known as "Fake it until you make it," that works well. I'm not suggesting you misrepresent yourself. I'm only suggesting that you begin to see yourself succeeding. Visualize your successes. See yourself vividly in your mind's eye making the sale and reaching your goals. Affirm over and over that you are succeeding. Write your affirmations daily. Of course, make sure you take the appropriate action to confirm your affirmations.

Remember that your subconscious mind does not know the difference between real and imaginary. Before each sales call, take a moment and mentally rehearse the scene, just like actors and athletes do. Tell yourself, "I'm a great salesperson." Do this over and over, especially just before a sales call. See the sale being made. See and feel the success. You will be pleasantly amazed at the result. Don't take my word for it. Give it a try. You have nothing to lose and everything to gain.

ED AND THE CAR

An amusing example of this idea is the story told to me by my friend Ed. Ed had just finished attending a sales training program where he was taught that just before calling on a prospective customer, in order to put himself in a peak mental and physical state, he should run around his car a few times.

Ed, anxious to use what he had learned, did this just before going in to see a new prospect at a major account. The meeting went well. The man liked Ed and his presentation and agreed to hire Ed's company.

The man was escorting Ed out of the building when he turned to Ed and said, "Ed, I have one question. I really like you and enjoyed your presentation and I feel good about working with your company, but I was wondering why were you running around your car in the parking lot?"

Apparently the man's office window faced the direction where Ed had parked his car. His important prospect had watched him making a fool of himself running around his car! Blushing, Ed told the man the story. They both had a good laugh, and Ed gained a new friend and customer.

DON'T BE AN ELEPHANT

It has been said throughout history that whatever you believe with conviction, you can achieve. Don't be like the poor elephant and go through your life stuck in one place because of a limiting belief you developed years ago. Take charge of your life and live it to the fullest. You deserve the best.

Where do beliefs come from? Like the elephant, we have been conditioned by our beliefs. Many times, these aren't even our own. Some originated from well-intentioned parents, teachers, and our peers while we were growing up.

For example, I was given the belief that I couldn't draw. A grade school art teacher did not like a picture I had drawn and told me that I had no artistic talent. Unfortunately, I believed her most of my life, and consequently have never enjoyed drawing or painting. A number of years ago I was able to disprove her assessment with the help of a book titled *Drawing on the Artist Within* by Betty Edwards. In it she proves that anyone can learn to draw well. I was given the same negative belief about my singing ability. Perhaps one day I will change that as well. If at some future date you attend one of my seminars and see a band on stage, you'll know why!

Fortunately for me, no one told me I couldn't write!

DREAM CRUSHERS

Often, without even realizing it, our friends and families instilled destructive limiting beliefs in us. For example, when discussing going into business for ourselves, many were met with comments like, "You can't do that," or "You'll never get ahead doing that," or "That's just a big scam, save your money." While these well-intentioned people were simply trying to prevent possible failure, they were actually undermining our self-esteem and limiting our potential for success.

That's why it's a good idea to be careful about who you share your dreams with, especially in the beginning. If you are starting a new business venture, beware of the dream crushers. There's another group of people you'll want to avoid, also. The not-so-well intentioned people who attempt to break our spirits because our success will force them to look at themselves and their own lack of accomplishment. Avoid all these naysayers!

HANG OUT WITH WINNERS

What about your new empowering beliefs? How do you strengthen them? Again I recommend you find references to support your new beliefs. One of the reasons 12-step programs are successful is that the newcomer sees other people who have successfully changed their behavior and have overcome their addiction.

If you want to change a limiting negative belief about the way you look, for example, seek out people who successfully changed their physical appearance and learn what they did. Uncover the beliefs, actions, and strategies that made them successful. Then model their behaviors.

I CAN'T BECAUSE...

Virtually all successful people believe they will succeed in whatever they do. They expect to succeed. They assume success as the natural outcome of their efforts. They project, affirm, and visualize their success. The real danger with a limiting belief is that it will prevent you from even trying in the first place. It's only natural then to want to change those limiting beliefs that stand between you and the life of your dreams.

The easiest and fastest way to change a belief is to challenge it. Our beliefs are held together by a supporting system of references. However, we can find references to support either side of a belief. We can find references to support the idea that politicians are crooks. There are enough of them in jail to support this belief. Or we can find references to support the opposite—that politicians are good and create positive change.

Whenever I give a workshop in a prison, I get the "I'll never get ahead because I'll always be an ex-convict" belief. I then tell the story of a local man who went from jail to a job as a car washer at an auto dealership. Because of his excellent attitude and belief in himself, he was then promoted to the service department. From there he went into sales and into sales management. Today he is a vice president with that organization.

At that point in my story, I ask who in the group knows of someone who got out of prison and was able to put their lives back together. Most of the hands in the group go up as the men realize that they *do* have a chance. I explain to them that if they believe they can succeed, they will. I tell them my own story and how I rose from a lowly lifestyle because I believed I could.

ANDY'S A WINNER

A more amazing story is about my friend Andy who, for most of his life, had the belief that his future was to be spent on a park bench drinking a bottle of wine. After all, he reasoned, that is all he had ever known. At one point he spent two years living in the Staten Island Ferry terminal in New York City. He thought this was a move up! Then he was offered a room at the Salvation Army, he entered into a treatment program, got off the booze and drugs, went to college, earned a degree, and the last time I saw him he had become a registered nurse and had a degree as a certified alcohol counselor.

I've known countless people who have changed their situation in life by first changing their belief as to what was possible. Whatever your story, trust that you can change your circumstances. It begins with changing your limiting beliefs.

Changing Your Beliefs Exercise

In your journal or below, write three limiting beliefs you now hold that you feel are preventing you from having what you want. They may be beliefs like: I don't have enough money to start a business, or I grew up poor so I can't get ahead, or I can never lose weight because I'm big boned. Whatever your limiting beliefs, choose three to five of them and write them down.

1.

2.

3.

Next, write three to five new beliefs that you want to develop. What would you like to believe? What kinds of new beliefs would help you have the kind of life you want? What new beliefs would serve your needs now? What do you need to believe about yourself to become the person you want to become?

1.

2.

3.

4.

5.

FAKE IT UNTIL YOU MAKE IT

Act as if you have already achieved your goals. Once you have completed the above exercise and identified your new empowering beliefs, you can begin to see yourself as being that person. You can act as if you have already become the person you want to be. For example, if you want to discard an old belief about being overweight, weak, and unhealthy and develop a new empowering belief that you are fit, strong, and healthy, you can begin by acting the way a fit person would act. When faced with food choices, for example ask yourself, "What would the person I want to become choose to eat?"

If you want to be a successful entrepreneur, see yourself as already successful. Dress and look your best at all times. Act successful. Once again, in any situation ask, "What would a successful person do in this situation?" "What would the person I want to become do in this situation?"

TRYING ON SUCCESS

Another way to reinforce your new image of affluence is to do little things that will give you a glimpse of a more affluent lifestyle. Go to the best hotel in town, even to just sit in the lobby or to have a cup of coffee in the cafe. Feel the opulence. Get comfortable in the surroundings. They're all there for you to enjoy. You could begin browsing in more expensive stores to help you become accustomed to your impending success.

If a new belief you want to cultivate is that of becoming a more loving parent and spouse, begin now by acting that way. Ask yourself, "How would a totally loving person handle this situation?" Do little things that will make you more loving. What would a loving person do for his or her family today? See yourself as being the new person you have decided to become. In a later chapter, we'll discuss visualization in more detail.

MY OLD CAR

Some time ago I had an old beat-up car and wanted a new car. Having learned the principles I'm writing about here, I went to the dealership and asked for a picture of the car I wanted. I had all the information necessary. I knew the price, options, colors, and every last detail of this automobile.

I took the picture and hung it above my desk where I would see it every day. I then went about my business, doing my work, not really paying much attention to the car although the picture was there for me to see as I worked.

A short time later, I had the exact car in my driveway. Like all other successful people, I had achieved my goal first in my mind and then in reality. Of course I worked to earn the money for it—the car dealer did not just come by and give me the car.

Remember, your subconscious mind does not know the difference between the real and the imagined. I can prove that. If I were to ask if you would be willing to walk across a plank that is 20 feet long and 18 inches wide and had a $100 bill at the other end, and I put that plank on the ground in front of you and asked you to walk across it and pick up the bill, you would probably be more than happy to do that, and you would have no problem with it. If, on the other hand, I were to take the same plank, the same $100 bill, the same length, but added one new dimension—moving the plank 50 stories into the air—you would probably not want to do it.

Logically, it's the same situation. It's the same plank, the same reward at the end of it. The only difference is that your imagination got involved. Your imagination became part of the equation.

LOGIC VERSUS IMAGINATION

When logic and imagination come into conflict, imagination wins. Fortunately, you can harness this power and use it to your advantage. Invest some time each day thinking about what you want. Make mental pictures of who you want to become, using as much detail as you can. Be sure to include colors, sounds, scents, and any other detail you can imagine.

Your subconscious mind does not know the difference between real and imagined. If you tell it over and over again that you are healthy and wealthy, it will believe you and direct you to the people, places, and things that will make this true for you.

AFFIRMATION

As you work with your affirmations, you will notice slight changes in your behavior. For example, you may notice that you are making healthier food choices or beginning to exercise. You may find yourself in a conversation about a business opportunity. These are the results of the work that you're doing internally. Be open to possibilities and trust that your Higher Power will guide you to your highest good. I suggest that you keep your affirmations simple, positive, and in the present tense.

In addition to "I approve of myself," you could write a simple affirmation that encompasses everything that you want to become. Something like, "Every day in every way I'm becoming better and better and better." This was suggested by Claude Bristol in his wonderful work, *The Magic of Believing,* which was written in 1948 and is one of the classics in self-help books.

I have used "I'm healthy, wealthy, and successful" as my main affirmation. You can then devise other affirmations to address each area you are working on. Be sure to write them daily, if possible, 25 or 30 times or more and use mirror work. Reciting your affirmations in a mirror is one of the most powerful tools that you can ever use and will speed your progress immensely.

Below is a list of affirmations to help you get started. You can choose one or two of these or write your own:

- I approve of myself.

- I allow myself to be successful.

- I deserve to win big.

- I live my life with ease and joy.

- I add value to everyone I meet.

- I take really good care of myself.

- I'm a winner.

- I'm happy, healthy, and successful.

- I'm fit and trim.

- I eat only foods that nourish me.

- Water is my fitness drink.

- I have total abundance in my life.

- I'm a wonderful, loving person.

- Lots of money is flowing into my life.

- I deserve all good.

- I'm relaxed and at peace.

TAKE A BREAK, YOU DESERVE IT

You have come a long way, my friend.

Now that you have:

- Identified the areas in your life you want to change

- Learned to accept and own everything in your life

- Developed a more positive attitude

- Identified your limiting beliefs, and

- Developed new, empowering ones…you deserve a break.

Take some time, a day or two, to let the material you have read take hold in your life. Congratulate yourself! You are on your way to a more exciting, fulfilling, and rewarding life.

Chapter 3

Decisions and Dreams

*It's a funny thing about life; if you refuse to accept
anything but the best, you very often get it.*
–Somerset Maugham

Everything you do—or for that matter, everything you
don't do—begins with a decision. You decide whether or
not to get out of bed in the morning. You decide what to
wear. You decide whether to go to work or not, what to do
when you get there, who to spend time with, and so on and
so on. Often these decisions are made unconsciously without much thought.

In the long run, the decisions you make or don't make
affect the direction of your life. You could decide to stay in
bed and not go to work. However, if you did this on a regular
basis, you wouldn't have a job to go to. Instead, you decide to
go to work in order to earn the money to have what you want
in your life.

In fact, everything in your life—your work, your relationships, your health—is a result of past decisions and choices.

If you want to make changes in your life (and who
doesn't?), you must first decide to do so. If you want better

health, decide right now to make a change. If you are in a dead-end job that you dread going to each day, decide right here and now to do something about it.

Decide to create the life you want and deserve. Today!

Change happens in an instant. All change is preceded by a decision. You can alter the direction of your life in an instant by deciding to change. Anyone who has ever succeeded in changing a habit of drinking, or eating, or smoking, or even drugs has, at some point, come to a place where they made a decision to change. It was during that moment of decision that the change began. Granted, it may have taken years to get to that point, but the decision to change occurred in a flash.

MY MOMENT OF TRUTH

In the introduction, I wrote about my story and how my life sank to the depths of poverty before I reached what I consider my "bottom." This took years to occur. The conditions in my life worsened little by little over a period of ten years. This is the way it happens to most people. Our lives slowly become worse without our even realizing how far down we've gone until one day we're at the bottom.

The journey to the bottom was slow and steady; however, the change, my moment of truth, occurred in a flash. I can remember the moment like it was yesterday, even though it was many years ago. I woke up in a hospital alcohol ward, my financial net worth about $3.85, my once promising life a disaster. I remember sitting on a worn-out sofa watching an

old television with a coat hanger for an antenna, thinking, *This is definitely not the Ritz Carlton.*

I clearly remember sitting there, my arms outstretched, looking up at the ceiling and saying to God, "I give up! Please either take me or help me. I can't go on like this."

That moment my life began to turn around. In that instant, my life changed. Something inside of me changed. I immediately felt a sense of hope and have never, from that moment on, had any craving for alcohol. The obsession to drink was lifted. This was the miracle in my life, and it happened in the blink of an eye. Of course the rebuilding process took some time and will continue throughout my life—but I had hope from that moment onward. There is always room to grow.

You can decide right here, right now, that you are going to make the changes you outlined in the first chapter when you completed the exercise. If you haven't done this exercise, please go back now and complete it.

DECIDE NOW

In your journal or in the back of this book, write a brief paragraph about what decisions you have made. Then date it and sign it. You might write something like this:

> Today, I have decided I will take charge of my health and no longer eat foods that are unhealthy for my body. I will pay attention to my food intake and eliminate those foods that don't nourish my body.

I have decided to begin my own part-time business in order to build a secure financial future. I will first investigate the opportunities available to me, choose one, and then pursue my new business to the best of my ability.

Once you have made the decision to change and to act, you are on your way to a better and more enjoyable life.

SEE IT FIRST

There is a wonderful story about the opening of Disney World in Orlando, Florida. A reporter who was interviewing Roy Disney, Walt Disney's brother, exclaimed, "It's too bad Walt did not live to see this." Roy quickly replied, "Walt saw it first. That's why you're seeing it now."

Walt Disney had a dream. He was one of the people who had not forgotten how to dream and to dream big. Walt knew that if he could imagine something, if he could dream it, he could make it a reality. The Disney empire is a true testimony of the effects of a vivid imagination and the benefits of following your dreams. Walt Disney didn't forget what it was like to be a child and took those imaginations and dreams to heart to create entertainment parks that thrill young and old alike.

Children have no trouble imagining and dreaming. If you ask children what they want for Christmas, you'll most likely be given a long list. Ask an adult the same question and you're likely to hear something like, "I don't know" or "Oh, anything is fine, I don't need much." Why do we as adults have such a hard time identifying what we want? Why do we believe it's our lot in life to simply accept whatever comes our way? Why are we afraid to dream and ask the universe for what we want?

YOU ARE DESERVING

Are you supposed to settle? Are you so undeserving? Do you really believe all the wonderful things and experiences here on earth are for someone else? If you believe that all of the glory and wonderment is here for you too, then you owe it to yourself to relearn how to dream.

What were you told? "Stop dreaming! Be realistic! Get your head out of the clouds! Be thankful for what you have!" Do any of these statements sound familiar to you? If you are like most, you heard these comments over and over from family members, teachers, and friends. While they may have been well-intentioned and meant to help us, they had the opposite affect.

Sure you should be grateful for what you have. As a matter of fact, affirming your gratitude and counting your blessings is a powerful exercise, and I recommend doing so on a daily basis. However, dreaming of a bigger and better future doesn't mean you're not grateful for what you have now. It just means you want an even better future!

Norman Vincent Peale said that if you want to have a big life, you need big dreams. If you want to have the kind of life you deserve, you need to begin dreaming again. Get back in touch with what you really want. What did you want as a child? What great dreams did you have that you may have forgotten? What do you want in your life now?

YOU HAVE A DREAM

Everything in our world—every new labor-saving device or invention, every breakthrough idea, every song ever sung, every book ever written, and every other accomplishment, large and small—began with a thought. Every great achievement was first a dream in the mind of the person who did it.

Martin Luther King Jr. had a dream, as did Gandhi, Mother Teresa, Walt Disney, Thomas Edison, Madame Curie, Henry Ford, Bill Gates, Ben & Jerry, Estee Lauder, Steve Jobs, George Lucas, Princess Diana, John F. Kennedy, Andrew Carnegie, Coco Chanel, and every great achiever since the beginning of time.

The life I lead today began in my imagination several years ago. I envisioned living in a home in the country surrounded by woods with my loving wife and making a difference, doing work that I love. Today I'm living that dream. I receive letters daily from people who have been inspired to action by something they read in one of my books or articles. I get to spend my days writing and speaking to people all around the world and have the opportunity to share what I have learned with them.

Of course, I now have new dreams. The more I accomplish, the more I have, the bigger my dreams become. It's part of the natural expansion of the universe.

MY MAGIC WAND

Pretend for a moment that I have a magic wand. Remember, I asked you to become like a child again. I'm going to wave this magic wand over your head, and you will be granted whatever you desire. This is a magic wand, so there are no limits. You can have whatever your heart desires. You can do whatever you want to do. You can be whatever you want to be.

There are no limits. What do you want? If there were no limits and you could manifest your dreams, all of them, what would that be? Would you want to climb the Matterhorn? Take a cruise to Alaska? Swim with dolphins? Sail the seas of the world? Have lunch atop the Eiffel Tower? Ride the Orient Express? Visit Disney World?

Do you want a new career? Your own business? Do you want to learn new skills? Play a musical instrument? Learn a foreign language? Get your degree? Learn a craft? Or perhaps, become a gourmet cook?

Would you like to become a better wife or husband? A more loving parent? A more spiritually connected person? Do you want more passion in your life? More excitement? More adventure?

Would a new car please you? What color? What make? How about a boat? Do you want a new house? A second home? New furniture? A stereo? A television? A camera? A computer? New carpeting? How about a new paint job?

Do you want to lose weight? Be healthier? Try a new hair style? Get braces to straighten your teeth? Be free of illness? Increase your energy?

Would you like more income? How much more? How about investments and savings? What would you do with an extra thousand dollars a month, or ten thousand dollars a month? Or even an extra hundred thousand dollars a month? Do you believe that's possible?

CLARITY IS KEY

There are people who earn that kind of money—lots of them. The fact is that they are people just like you and me. The only difference is that they have become clear as to what they want in their lives and have taken action toward achieving their goals. It's interesting to note that many highly successful people are making major contributions to society. They're the ones who are giving the most and are receiving the most as well.

What are your dreams? What do you want? You can have whatever you want in this life. All of your dreams can come true. It's really a matter of deciding what you want and becoming willing to do something to have it.

Your Dreams Exercise

In your journal or in the back of the book, write your dream sheet. Write down everything you want to do, to be, to have, and to share in your life. Remember, this is a magic wand exercise so don't worry about how you will accomplish these things. For now, all you want to do is gain some insight into what you really want. List everything you can think of, no matter how outrageous. Later we will zero in on what's really important to you.

What do you want? Don't let your logical mind get involved and start editing. Ignore the little voice that's saying, "You can't do that" or "You can't have that, it's too expensive." Ignore it! Tell that little voice to be quiet just for now.

Logic and reason have their place, but not in a dreaming or brainstorming exercise. Most people never realize their potential because they let their reasoning mind talk them out of things before they even begin.

Here's what happens. You think to yourself, *I'd like a new luxury automobile.* Before you even have a chance to settle in with the desire, your logical mind interrupts with something like, *Don't be foolish. Where will you get the money?* If you learn to ignore your reasoning mind for a while and just go with the dream, you may learn that there are many ways to accomplish your goal of a new car. You could, for example, get a job as a salesperson in an automobile dealership and have a demo car to use. You may even win a car. Or you could earn the necessary money and simply buy it. The point is to let your creative mind work on the desire before your logical mind dismisses it as frivolous.

GENIUS OR LUNATIC?

Many years ago, Walt Disney had an idea for an amusement park. People told him he was crazy, that he couldn't charge admission simply to go into a park; furthermore, the idea of an amusement park for adults was totally unheard of.

Fortunately, a banker at Bank of America in California believed in Walt Disney and lent him the money to build Disneyland. Amazingly, the entire loan was paid back during the first year of operation. Wow!

Write down everything that you can imagine having and becoming in your life. My friend Jack Canfield, co-author of the incredibly successful *Chicken Soup for the Soul* series, suggests in *The Aladdin Factor,* another wonderful book he co-authored, that you write down 101 wishes.

Take a couple of pages in your journal, or in the back of the book, and write the numbers 1 to 101. I promise that once you have completed this exercise, you'll have uncovered pretty much everything you could possibly want in your life.

Chapter 4

Goals

There are two ways to face the future. One way is with apprehension; the other is with anticipation.
–Jim Rohn

When you go on vacation, do you stand patiently in an airport ticket line, step up to the counter, plop down your suitcase and say to the agent, "I want to go on a vacation, please sell me a ticket to somewhere"? Of course not. By the time you and your family leave for vacation, you have probably been planning it for months. You have decided and agreed upon where you want to go, developed your schedule, made travel and hotel arrangements, obtained brochures about the places you want to visit, picked out some attractions you want to see and special things you want to do there. You have most likely been talking about the trip, even seeing yourselves there doing the things you want to do.

Maybe you've been counting down the days until departure time, your excitement building until the "final moments." You and your family have probably "visited" there in your minds time and time again. Finally, the day arrives and you head off on your long-awaited, carefully

planned, vividly imagined, constantly affirmed and rein-
forced family vacation.

"Wow, this is great," you say, as you actually experience
the feeling you have imagined all along. It's even better than
you imagined.

If you were willing to put all that effort into planning
your vacation, why then do you leave your life to chance?
Why do you get up in the morning, shower, get dressed, walk
out the door, and just "wing it"? Surely your life deserves at
least as much attention as your vacation!

Most people go through each day having no idea what
they want or where they're going. It's a sad fact that most of
us invest more time and energy into planning our vacations
than planning our lives.

You, my friend, aren't one of these people. If you were,
you wouldn't have picked up this book in the first place. No,
you want more. The fact that you've read this far demonstrates that you want lifelong success.

In my opinion and in the opinion of many others, setting
goals is the pivotal point on the path to success and happiness. Earl Nightingale, the famous motivational speaker and
author, said it best when he defined success as, "The progres-
sive achievement of a worthwhile goal."

Zig Ziglar, one of the most significant success coaches of
our time, reminds us that we "cannot return from a vacation
we have not taken, and we cannot reach a goal we have not
set." My feeling is that if you haven't defined what success
means to you and have no measurable goals, how can you

know if you are successful? If you don't know what success looks like, you won't recognize it when it shows up! It has been said that a person without a goal is like a ship without a rudder. I've always liked the analogy of a piece of Styrofoam bouncing around the ocean, moving in whatever direction the wind and waves take it. This is no way to live your life. Set goals!

PURPOSE AND RESULTS

Many years ago, a friend of mind defined purpose as "a reason to expend energy." Purpose gives us a reason to get out of bed in the morning. It keeps us going in the face of adversity. It gives us the inner strength we need to overcome any obstacle. If your purpose or goal is strong enough, you will find a way. Our goals help us answer the question, "Why am I doing this?"

A while back I had reached the point where I had to take some action toward improving my physical health and fitness. I was tired of the way I looked and felt. I had gained weight and had low energy most of the time. Sound familiar? I decided I had to change.

Following the steps I cover in this book and in my seminars, I set a goal to get in shape, to reach a specific weight by a specific date, and change some of my eating habits, eliminating certain foods from my diet. As part of my action plan (we will discuss this in the next chapter), I joined a health club. My goal was to work out between four and five times each week. My purpose was clear. I was on my way to victory!

One bitter cold winter day with the temperature below zero, my resolve was put to the test. In order to keep to my schedule and my commitment that particular week, I needed to go to the gym at 6 A.M. on a day that was brutally cold. The only reason I was on a treadmill at 6:05 A.M. that freezing day is that I had clearly defined my goal and had become committed to achieving it. My purpose was clear.

Your purpose will get you through the tough (or cold) times. An added benefit is the power you feel from having overcome the tendency to lie in bed under the warm blankets.

Your purpose is the reason behind your goal. Your purpose is why you want the goal in the first place.

In the 1960s, President John F. Kennedy set a national goal to put a man on the moon before the end of the decade. This was not because he wanted to learn if there really was green cheese on the moon! His purpose and the reason he succeeded was to ensure that the United States would remain a world power and not take a back seat in the race into space.

It's interesting to note that when he set that particular goal, President Kennedy had no idea how it would be reached. He did, however, have the other necessary ingredients for success:

- The belief that it could be done

- The commitment to make it happen

- The willingness to take action, in this case, massive action

Others were inspired by his goal and made it their own. In 1969, all the world watched their televisions as the first human, an American named Neil Armstrong, walked proudly on the surface of the moon. All successful people have clear goals.

OUR HOME

Several years ago my wife, Georgia, and I were house hunting. Several factors were making it difficult to find a suitable house. Among them was the fact that our home was described as "hard to sell." One day after returning from yet another unsuccessful day of house hunting, I watched my wife break into tears. I pulled the car over to the side of the road and tried to comfort her. I understood her frustration and shared her feelings.

Then something inside me clicked. I said, "Wait a minute. We're doing this all wrong," remembering my experiences and what I had learned. I said, "Let's do what I suggest in my writing. Instead of being concerned with selling our present house, let's focus on what we want, not on what we don't want, and go from there. Let's set a goal and take the appropriate action."

We decided that our anniversary, October 27, would be our goal cut-off date. We wrote it down and went on about our business. Every few weeks, we would go look at more houses, with no success.

Months passed, and frankly I was beginning to wonder about the effectiveness of this goal-setting stuff myself. As our anniversary approached, we had planned to visit upstate New York for a few days, and then on the day of our anniversary go to Bucks County in Pennsylvania. Our New York trip was not what we wanted, so we called the bed and breakfast where we were scheduled to stay and asked to arrive a few days early. Keep in mind that we were "supposed" to be in upstate New York.

The day before our anniversary, we were driving from one location to another looking at vacant lots. We had decided that if we couldn't locate the house we needed, we could always have it built. During our drive to the next location, I glanced to my right and saw some huge homes being built. My first thought was, "They're too expensive," but Georgia suggested we stop anyway on the way back.

We did stop and spoke with the builder. It turned out they were within our price range. The hitch was there was only one lot that was suitable for us and we did not know if it would work. We needed to build a walk-out basement for Georgia's parents' apartment.

This was one day before the target date to reach our goal! Our original plans had us a hundred miles away on that day but here we were. The arrangement worked out, and today we live in a beautiful custom-built home—a goal realized and truly a dream come true. No one will ever tell me goal-setting doesn't work. I know better!

LANDMARK STUDY

You may have heard about the classic landmark study that was done at a major university in the 1950s. Researchers interviewed the graduating class and found that only 3 percent had written goals with plans for their achievement. They followed this group for 20 years. In 1974 or 1975 when they reinvestigated the group, they found that in measurable areas, specifically financial success, the three percent who had written down their goals were financially worth more than the other 97 percent combined.

GOAL-SETTING—THE MECHANICS

The following are some guidelines for writing your goals:

1. Your goals must be written in the present tense (I have, I am, I allow, I earn, etc.). Your subconscious mind takes things literally. It does not respond to past or future tenses. Writing something like, "I will be having..." will instruct your subconscious mind to keep the goal out of reach—in the future.

2. Your goals must be stated in the positive. Writing "I will lose 20 pounds" won't work as well if it works at all. Your subconscious mind cannot work on the reverse of an idea. Negative commands like can't, won't, don't, lose, etc., aren't interpreted by your subconscious mind.

For example, if I say to you, "Don't think of a pink elephant," what happens? If I say, "Think of anything you want but don't think of a pink elephant," you immediately think of a pink elephant, right? It's the same with your goals. Keep them in the positive. Rather than, "I will lose 20 pounds," you could write, "On or before (date), I am at my ideal weight of 120 pounds."

3. When dealing with goals that can be measured (weight, finance, etc.), be as specific as possible and have a target date. For example, a goal of "more money" is not likely to produce much of a result; it's too vague. A better way to put it would be, "I enjoy owning my own part-time business and earning an additional $1,000 per month on or before July 1."

ONE STEP AT A TIME

It's a good idea to set goals for different timeframes. Short, medium, and long-range goals all help to give our lives a sense of direction and work together to help us have the life of our dreams. An added benefit of shorter range goals is that the thrill of accomplishing them helps us stay motivated. If all you had were long-range goals, it would be difficult to measure your progress and harder to keep yourself going in the face of setbacks. Personally, I like to set short–term (3-6 months); one-year; medium-term (3-5 years); and long-term (10-20 year) goals.

That last one, the 20-year goal, I learned from Robert Schuller and it has been a real challenge to project my life out 20 years into the future. While circumstances will change, having a general idea of where I'm going makes my life more meaningful. Of course, I modify these goals as I go along and circumstances change.

Chances are you will be there in 20 years. The big question is where will "there" be? What will your life be like in 20 years? What will you be doing? Who will you be? By dreaming it now and taking appropriate action, you can begin to create the life you will want to be living 20 years from now.

By working backward, you can begin to take the necessary actions today to take you where you want to go. For example, if one of your long-range goals is financial independence with enough passive income—income you don't have to labor for, like residual income, investment income, royalties, etc.—for the rest of your life, you will see that one of your short-term goals needs to be beginning an investment program, establishing your own business, or doing something that will enable you to create these passive income streams.

BEWARE OF SELF-SABOTAGE

Some people avoid writing and setting goals because they're afraid they won't reach them. So what! If you don't set goals you surely won't reach them because you won't have them in the first place.

There are ways to change this self-defeating thinking. First, make sure your goals are within reach for the time period you set. A goal of being 20 pounds lighter by next Thursday is not likely to work unless you are giving birth to a baby! Give yourself sufficient time to accomplish the goal. Goals should, however, be a stretch for you. Don't make them too easy. You want to challenge yourself and "push the envelope" to stretch out of your comfort zone. Second, if you miss a goal, move the date or rewrite the goal. They are written in your journal, not carved in stone!

By setting goals, writing them down and taking action, you will succeed. You are already ahead of 97 percent of the population. Just by having set your goals your likelihood of succeeding increases greatly. Even if you don't fully reach your goal, you will have made more progress and accomplished more than if you had not set goals in the first place.

This past year, I set a goal to read two books each month. My plan was to read each day and by the end of the year to have read 24 books. Well, things changed. My circumstances changed and my schedule became heavier. There were many days when I shortened my reading time.

Interestingly enough, because I had set a goal, I ended the year having read 19 books. Though I missed my original target goal, I'm far better off than if I had not set it in the first place. By the way, I did not factor in the dozens of audio cassettes I listened to throughout the year. This year, my goal will include audio books too, and the goal will be higher.

If you set a goal to increase your income by $3,000 a month and only succeed in increasing it by $2,000, have you failed? Will you give the money back? Not likely. You are still way ahead of where you would be if you had not set the goal in the first place.

If you take only one thing from this book, let it be goal-setting. Having written goals and plans to achieve is one of the most powerful ideas you will ever use. Goals are magical. They have a way of coming true—sometimes in the strangest ways, but they do come true.

Goal-setting Exercise

Find a comfortable place where you won't be disturbed for a while. Allow sufficient time to complete this exercise. It may be one of the most important things you ever do. In your journal, or in the back of the book, set aside several pages for writing your goals. Go back to the exercise in the first chapter and look at the different areas of your life. Be sure to set goals in all these areas.

Go to the dream sheet exercise you completed earlier. This is where you wrote all your dreams and aspirations. Using this list as a guide, pick the ones that are most important to you. You may want to begin with the short-term and one-year goals for now and work up to the longer range ones.

Write one or two short-term goals from each category on a page or two. Be sure to leave space between them. Under each goal, write a short sentence about why you want this goal. What will having it mean to you? What will you get by reaching it? Go back to the exercise on commitment and use that as a guide. The more reasons you have for wanting the goal, the more likely you will do what is necessary to reach it. Do this for each of your short-term and one-year goals. Later you can come back and complete this for longer term goals.

Chapter 5

Energy and Enthusiasm

Nobody grows old merely by living a number of years. We grow old by deserting our ideals. Years may wrinkle the skin, but to give up enthusiasm wrinkles the soul. –Samuel Ullman

How many times do you come home from work, eat dinner, and plop down on the couch in front of the television because you're too tired to do anything else? Maybe you even eat in front of the TV. Unlike the Energizer Bunny, do your batteries run down around three o'clock in the afternoon? Are you just too beat to do anymore?

To have an exciting and productive life, to live your dreams and reach your goals, you will need abundant amounts of energy. It takes energy and physical health to enjoy life to the fullest. Unfortunately, most of our society lacks both the physical health and the stores of energy required to live fully. Too many of us, even children, lack the physical capacity to live the kind of life we want and deserve. Americans in particular are in such poor health and so unfit it has become a global embarrassment.

The good news is that it's never too late to change your physical condition. While you may have physical challenges that you cannot do anything about, there's always room for improvement in your overall condition. If you want proof of this, all you have to do is watch the Special Olympics and see how people with serious physical challenges have persevered regardless of their condition. Beginning from where you are, decide now to take better care of your physical health.

YOU ARE WHAT YOU EAT

While there have been enough books written about what to eat and what not to eat to fill a good-size bookstore, I would like to offer one simple suggestion on this subject. Whether you prefer to follow a diet of vegetarian, herbivore, fruitarian, or as one person put it, "an omnivore" (that's someone who eats whatever they want), there is a simple rule of thumb that will help you maintain a healthier food program. Simply obtain 70-80 percent of your food from fruits and vegetables. If you do this, you will automatically become healthier. Of course, you need to apply common sense as well.

In their series of *Fit for Life* books, Harvey and Marilyn Diamond explain this concept by pointing out that we are made up of 70-80 percent water. For that matter, our entire planet is 70-80 percent water. So it stands to reason that eating water-rich foods such as fruits and vegetables is good for us. One easy way to reach this level of water-rich foods is to eat a large, fresh salad with each meal.

Another key is moderation. A doctor once suggested to me that if I really wanted to have ice cream, go ahead, but have it once a week, not every night. This was something I was able to do without too much trouble.

AN APPLE A DAY

Another great suggestion is to eat an apple or two in the morning instead of a big breakfast. I know there is a lot of controversy about breakfast being an important meal, but modern research doesn't support that. Personally, I find an apple or two works great. There is enough sugar (glucose) to give my brain the nourishment it needs, and apples are low in fat. Over the course of a few years, I have found this to work well as long as I eat a light lunch early in the day. A fringe benefit is that apples are easy to eat on the run, a practice that many of us have adopted in our busy lifestyles.

An apple a day helps us to remain healthy because, among other things, apples contain large quantities of malic acid, a substance that helps fight bacteria and aids digestion. The old adage that "An apple a day keeps the doctor away" did not just become a cliché for no reason. Of course I occasionally have an egg breakfast complete with muffins or bagel because life is meant to be enjoyed, right?

If you're really serious about having better health, it's worthwhile to learn about nutrition. Your health is critical and it warrants professional advice to assist you in living the healthiest life you can. By all means have regular checkups with a qualified medical professional.

PHYSICAL EXERCISE

No discussion about energy would be complete without bringing up exercise. No doubt you've heard the expression, "Use it or lose it!" A simple exercise program, one that will keep your body reasonably fit and your heart working well, does not take a lot of time and can be enjoyable. Recent studies suggest that a person is better off being fit and overweight than not fit and thin. The key is to find an activity or several activities you enjoy and develop a regular routine.

One of the best and simplest overall fitness programs is simply to take a walk for 30-40 minutes several times a week. It costs nothing and does not require special equipment. You may even want to consider a personal trainer to help you design a program that's right for you. One word of caution—begin any exercise routine slowly; and to prevent injury, never force your body. Of course, see your medical professional before beginning any exercise program.

LEARN TO BREATHE

When was the last time you took a really deep breath? If you are like most people, breathing is something you take for granted. We assume we're breathing correctly but that's not necessarily true. Most people have a very shallow breathing pattern, and this can add to our everyday stress. When we get anxious, we tend to take short, rapid breaths. Critically acclaimed health expert, Dr. Andrew Weil, said that if he only had the time to teach a patient one thing, he would teach them proper breathing.

One way to relax under pressure is to purposely slow your breathing and take long, deep breaths. Some time ago, a friend taught me a breathing technique that has been very useful for reducing my stress. It's something I can use at any time during the day if I feel a bit tense.

The technique itself is simple. All you need do is take slow, steady breaths. Inhale to a count of five and exhale slowly to the same count. Do this five or ten times. If you're going to try this, please remember not to strain at any time and to stop if you feel dizzy or light-headed.

BE STILL

Much has been written about the benefits of meditation and quiet time. It reduces stress, speeds healing, lowers your heart rate, and can help you stay centered. All you really need to do is sit quietly for 20 minutes or so each day. Simply focus your attention on your breathing and quietly follow your breath as it enters and leaves your body. If your mind wanders and begins to focus on your chores or worries, gently bring it back and watch your breathing. Do this in a quiet place where you won't be interrupted. If you want to learn more about this, there are plenty of books, CDs, and classes to help you.

SET YOUR PRIORITIES

Your physical and mental health and well-being are at the center of your life. You can't feel successful if you are physically tired or stressed out. Make your health the #1 priority.

Many people sabotage themselves because they try to squeeze meditation and exercise into their busy schedules. If you want to succeed, rearrange your lifestyle to accommodate your wellness routines. Make it the most important thing on your "to do" list. Whatever your present physical condition, you can make small daily improvements and over time, look, feel, and be significantly healthier and happier. Go for it. You deserve it.

ENTHUSIASM AND EXCITEMENT

Get excited about life. As the title of this book asks and states, *What Are You Waiting For? It's Your Life!* Be enthusiastic.

I remember sitting in an office one day waiting for an appointment when a secretary covered her typewriter and with a big sigh proclaimed, "Well I made it through another day." I thought to myself, *How sad.* It was almost as if she was just checking off the days one by one until her life was over. Is this any way to live? I think not. I know you don't want to live life like this or you wouldn't be reading this book. Life is meant to be enjoyed. Life is exciting. If you don't believe me, watch small children as they discover the world around them.

One sunny summer afternoon I had the wonderful experience of taking a walk with a friend's three-year-old child. I had not been around a small child for quite some time and had forgotten how much children enjoy life. There is no such thing as ordinary or routine for a three or four year old. They see the wonderment in all of life. I remember at one point we stopped to watch an insect cross the sidewalk. On another occasion we stopped to examine the cracks in the sidewalk.

Nothing escaped this little child. All of life was exciting and interesting.

RIGHT HERE, RIGHT NOW

Children are more enthusiastic because they live in the present moment. They aren't beating themselves up about mistakes they made yesterday, nor are they worried about tomorrow. A three year old does not say, "I wish when I was two I knew what I know now." They are right here, right now.

The more we remind ourselves about being here—now—the happier and more successful we will be. Learn to be in the present moment. Each morning, ask yourself, *How can I make the most of this precious day?* The more I stay centered in the now, the better I feel and the more I accomplish.

The times when I "spin my wheels" are those times when I lapse into trying to change something beyond my control, like the past or fretting about some future event. Live today. I once read a little poem that helps me to remember this:

Yesterday is history

Tomorrow is a mystery

Today is a gift

That's why it's called the present!

STOP AND SMELL THE ROSES

How much of the joy and beauty of life do you stop and notice each day? Do you see the majestic sunrise as the light radiates across the early morning sky? Do you take in the freshness of the early morning air and bask, even if just for a moment, in the beauty of a newborn day? Or are you too busy getting ready for work? Do you, as they say, take time to stop and smell the roses?

There has never been a person who, on their death bed, said they wished they had spent more time at the office. Take the time to enjoy your life. Make a practice of noticing the small, everyday sights and sounds in your world.

What about your work? Are you excited and enthusiastic about what you do? Or are you like the secretary in my example who was just trying to make it through the day? Too many people in our society, as Henry David Thoreau said, are "leading lives of quiet desperation."

WAKE UP!

Get excited about your life. When someone asks you how you are, rather than simply saying okay or fine, try saying, "Great!" Say it with enthusiasm and you will be amazed at how often you will begin to feel better as a result of doing this.

Move and walk with enthusiasm. Put some bounce in your step and stand tall. It's your life. Live it with zest!

Try jumping out of bed in the morning with expectancy for the coming day instead of dragging yourself up complaining. Look to each day as the gift that it is.

Questions Exercise

If you read my first book, *Handbook to a Happier Life,* you may remember the section about morning questions. These are questions you develop to help put you in a positive frame of mind. Ask questions like:

- What am I excited about today?

- What am I looking forward to today?

- What am I grateful for?

- What makes me happy?

Find something in your work to excite you. Find something you are looking forward to experiencing every day and focus on that for a few minutes before you arise. Doing this will help put you in a positive, expectant, and enthusiastic state of mind.

Remember, your questions determine what you focus on, and your focus determines the quality of your experiences. For example, if you are walking down the street in a large city, you can choose to focus on the beauty of the tall buildings or you can choose to focus on the dirt and litter. Your choice greatly affects your experience of that city.

Likewise, you can choose to allow energy and enthusiasm into your life by focusing on the beauty in your world.

Chapter 6

Fear and Faith

You may be deceived if you trust too much, but you
will live in torment if you do not trust enough.
–Dr. Frank Crane

If you are to have the kind of life you want and deserve, you must learn to overcome your fears. Fear is the single biggest destroyer of dreams and has prevented more people from having what they want than any other factor. It prevents you from taking the actions necessary for your success and can keep you stuck right where you are.

When operating from a position of fear, we tense up, reducing the blood flow to our brain, which further complicates the situation. Now, not only are we in a fearful state, our thinking and ability to solve our problem is greatly hindered. I cannot emphasize enough how important it is to learn to break through, go around, go over or under, or whatever it takes to move past fear and into action. There are clearly actions we can take in any situation, and we must be willing to take them.

NATURAL FEARS

It's interesting to note that we are born with only two fears. The fear of loud noises and the fear of falling. All other fears are learned. We often tell children not to do certain things for fear they could be hurt. Sometimes this is good, like teaching a child not to venture out into traffic.

However, sometimes with the best of intentions, we become overly protective and can actually stifle the child's natural curiosity. As we grow from children into adults, we carry our fears with us and can develop a habit of not trying new things or of not deviating from the status quo. As adults, our reluctance to try new things is actually our fear of failure.

If you never take a risk, you cannot fail. Unfortunately, you cannot succeed either. In order to become the person you are capable of becoming, there will be times when you will need to take small, calculated risks. To live the kind of life you deserve, you will need to face your fears and take action to overcome them.

Fears tend to fall into one of three categories: the fear of failure, the fear of being hurt, and the fear of not being perfect. I realize the last one, the fear of not being perfect, may sound a bit strange, but many times we won't attempt something because we are holding on to a belief that we must be perfect in everything we do. We have been conditioned to be overly critical of ourselves and to expect unrealistic performance and results when we are, as the Billy Joel song so aptly points out, only human.

Have you chosen not to participate in an activity because you felt as though you were "not good enough"? Do you avoid dancing, singing, playing a sport, or public speaking simply because you feel a need to be perfect before you even attempt it?

The irony is that the way people become great at these activities is by doing them. The easiest way to overcome the fear of not being perfect is by allowing yourself to be less than perfect. Give yourself permission to feel uncomfortable with an activity until you have done it long enough to have acquired the skills needed to do it well. Don't let your perfectionism prevent you from partaking in and enjoying the many activities life has to offer. Do you really believe that everything Van Gogh, Dali, or DaVinci painted was brilliant? It's unlikely. I'm sure if you look at their early attempts you will see less-than-great art.

Did Billy Joel or Elton John jump out of their cribs and start writing hit songs? Their beginning efforts were probably not worth recording. As a matter of fact, Billy Joel once felt so much a failure that he considered taking his own life. Fortunately, he sought help and went on to become one of the most successful songwriters of our time.

When you were a child, did you just get up one day and start walking? I doubt it. You most likely crawled first, then began a ritual of standing, stumbling, and falling. After a period of trial and error you finally succeeded. The fact that you can walk today is only because you were willing to be "less than perfect" in your early attempts. So the next time the music starts playing, come out dancing.

FEAR OF FAILURE

When you do that which you fear, the death of fear is certain.

In *Handbook to a Happier Life*, I wrote, "There is no such thing as failure. Every action produces a result." Think about it. Whatever you are attempting to do, if you take an action, you will produce a result. It may not be the result you were looking for, but it will be a result nonetheless.

Too many times we let our fear of "failure" prevent us from taking any action at all. This is especially true for people who are considering starting their own business. The question, "What if I fail?" pops up immediately. Somehow we convince ourselves we won't succeed even before we begin. This is, however, understandable because most of us have been conditioned to think like this.

Most, if not all, successful entrepreneurs have had setbacks along the way. The difference is that they view their setbacks as learning experiences and temporary, while unsuccessful people consider the same outcomes as failures and give up before they even have a chance to succeed.

If you reframe a so-called "failure" and see it for what it really is—a temporary setback or learning experience—you will increase your chances of success.

GREAT FAILURES

When Thomas Edison was asked, after finally succeeding in inventing the electric light after about 10,000 attempts, what it was like to fail all those times he replied, "I did not fail. I simply discovered thousands of ways that wouldn't produce electric light." On another occasion, he quipped that he succeeded because he had exhausted all of the ways that wouldn't work.

Sometimes the result you produce by overcoming your fear of failure can be even more than you expected. Christopher Columbus set out to find a shortcut to India only to discover a New World. Was he a failure?

THREE-STEP SOLUTION

To break through your fear of failure, there is a three-step solution to remember:

1. Take action

2. Gauge the result

3. Modify your action

When you follow this three-step solution, you will achieve the result you want.

Consider that an airplane flying from San Francisco to the island of Maui is off course about 90 percent of the time. Comforting, isn't it? In reality, it's not a problem since the plane's computer is constantly making minor corrections in the flight path until the plane lands safely in Hawaii. Being off track is part of the process and is quite natural.

You can do the same. By gauging the results of your actions, eliminating what is not working, and emphasizing what works, you can produce the results you're looking for. This applies as much to health and fitness or relationships as it does to venturing into your own business.

THE FEAR OF BEING HURT

Your fear of being hurt, bumped, bruised, embarrassed, laughed at, or just having your ego dented is another fear that you need to overcome if you want to become all you are capable of becoming.

You'll never know your true potential or live your life to the fullest if you're not willing to risk some small hurts, real or imagined. I'm not suggesting that you put yourself in danger of being physically harmed or that you gamble everything you have and risk financial ruin. I'm referring to those "little" hurts—usually to our egos—that come from stepping out of our comfort zone and taking risks.

Here's an example from my own experience as an author. When I was writing my first book, I was in a very comfortable, nonthreatening space called writing a book. I could tell people, "I'm writing a book." It was safe and secure. It sounded cool. I couldn't be rejected as long as I remained in the writing stage. Unfortunately, unless I was willing to risk rejection, I would be the only person who would ever read what I was writing!

In order to experience all of the wonderful feelings and victories that come from being a successful author, I had to step out of my comfort zone and publish the book. As long as I was in the writing stage, I was very safe. However, in order to succeed, I had to risk. Fortunately for me, *Handbook to a Happier Life* has been a huge success, and I have experienced that wonderful feeling that comes from knowing that people are using something I wrote to make positive changes in their own lives.

BREAKING THROUGH FEAR

Feel your fear and move on. To simplify the process, let me suggest the following:

1. Face your fears. You cannot deny your fear. If you have a fear of telephoning people you don't know, which may be a definite disadvantage in your business, you need to acknowledge it and take steps to overcome it.

2. Analyze the fear.

   - What fear is stopping you from having what you want?

   - What is the worst that can happen if you go for it?

   - How likely is that to happen?

   - Can you live with it if it did?

3. Visualize success. See your action producing a successful outcome.

4. Break the pattern. Do something. Get up and move around the room. Sing, jump up and down, do something physical for a few minutes to increase your energy.

5. Go for it. Once you are feeling more powerful, pick up the phone and start dialing. Once you're in the process, the fear will dissipate. While you may never learn to enjoy calling total strangers on the telephone (few people do), you will have interrupted the fear long enough to get past it.

YOU CAN'T LOSE WHAT YOU DON'T HAVE

One last thought on the subject of fear. Many times people will avoid doing something for fear they won't succeed when, in reality, if they did not succeed, they would be no worse off than they are.

Let me explain. You're at a party and, across the room, you see that "perfect" person. You want to go over and ask her to dance but hesitate because you're afraid she will say no. Think about this for a moment. If you were to go over and ask the person to dance and she said no, where would you be? You'd be exactly where you are—not dancing! You wouldn't have lost anything. You can't lose what you don't have.

In business, when you let your fears prevent you from asking for an order, the situation is the same. If I'm not your customer now and you ask me for an order and I say no, I'm still not your customer. You haven't given up anything other than a slight bump to your ego, which you'll get over.

Remember: "If you don't ask, the answer is always no!"

FAITH

The best way to overcome fear is to develop a strong, unshakable faith. There is a wonderful little truth about faith: Fear knocked on the door. When faith answered, there was no one there.

Faith is that sense of knowing, even though you cannot yet see the result, that everything will work out for your own highest good. Faith is the inner "knowing" that you will achieve your desired result in any undertaking. It's believing, even though you have no proof. It's trusting and becoming as a child in your trust. Trust your inner guidance.

There have been many times in my past when I was stuck and didn't know what to do next. At these times perhaps we all experience a test of our faith. When faced with these challenges, I focus on my goal and take action. From my experience, it is clear to me that the key is have faith in your abilities and skills, take action, and trust that it will all work out.

Sometimes we may feel we don't have enough faith or any at all for that matter. That is nonsense. Think about all the acts of faith you perform each day. In its simplest form, you demonstrate faith each time you exhale. You don't worry about where your next breath will come from, do you? Yet, we worry about where the rent money or car payment will come from.

I have been in that situation more times than I'd like to remember, and looking back, I now realize that whenever things didn't work out, it was because I wasn't taking action on my faith.

When I became willing to act and did what I intuitively felt was the right action, everything worked out fine.

We don't fret that the sun will rise tomorrow. We have the trust and faith that it will. We drive our automobiles down two-lane roads at 60 miles per hour and trust that the other cars will remain on their side of the dividing line. We don't question. We just have faith that it will all work out, and it usually does. Why then do you worry needlessly about the rest of your life?

If you are doing what you feel in your heart is right, and you are taking care of your part in the play (as Shakespeare said), then simply know that all is well.

What I have found to be fascinating is that what we ask for becomes manifest because of our faith that it will. If you set out to achieve a result, whether it's in health, business, relationships, finance, education, or your spiritual life, and you know deep in your heart that something will occur and you hold to that unshakable faith, it will come to pass.

Your success is directly proportional to your faith in your ability to succeed.

Chapter 7

Choices and Commitment

*Our grand business in life is not to see what lies dimly
at a distance, but to do what lies clearly at hand.*
–Thomas Carlyle

As we walk down the pathway of our lives, we are constantly
making choices—good and not so good—that affect where
we are going. As Yogi Berra, the great baseball star and American philosopher said to a graduating class at Harvard, "As you
go through life you will come to a fork in the road. Take it."

I think people like Yogi, while he had little formal education, are profound in their observations of life. We make
choices all day long. What to wear, where to go, what to eat,
who to be with, and on and on. Many of these choices we
make unconsciously, operating more out of habit than anything else.

How many times have you been in a restaurant at lunch-
time and when the waiter asked what you wanted you said
without much thought, "Oh, I'll have a burger, fries, and a
soda." Did you stop and ask yourself what you really wanted,
or better yet what would be most nourishing to your body?
Probably not. You probably ordered something out of habit.

What about at work? Do you keep making the same choices simply because they are familiar? Imagine for a moment what would happen if you made some new choices; what if you ordered a lunch that would really feed your body instead of weighing it down with high fat, high sugar, high cholesterol food? Suppose for a moment that at work you made new choices based on what would be more effective, creative, or productive. How would that feel? Imagine coming home from work and choosing to spend quality time with your family instead of turning on the television or surfing the Internet.

What about the possibility of making totally new choices for your work? Well-known inspirational speaker Zig Ziglar has commented that if you go to a job today simply because you went there yesterday, you might want to reconsider your choices.

RETHINK

Begin evaluating the choices you make in your daily living. Question whether or not they are guiding you where you want to go. Write in your journal some new choices you could be making and then go and make them. If you are in a financial rut and want to get out, how might you make new choices to accomplish this?

What about trading television time for a new business opportunity? You could begin a part-time business with an investment of a couple of hours each evening and build it into a full-time enterprise that could very well provide you with financial independence and wealth.

If you want to lose weight, you could choose to go for a walk rather than eat dessert. Do you want more communication and harmony in your family? Why not model what some families are doing and set aside one evening each week when all family members are present, spending time together talking and sharing their feelings. Some families invite guests and have found the evenings have become a popular social event.

By becoming aware of the choices we make on a daily basis, we can choose those foods, activities, and situations that will help us create the kind of life we want and deserve to have. It's the small, seemingly insignificant choices we make daily that mold who we become. Your life today is the sum total of the choices you've made up to this point. To change your life, make some new choices.

CONSCIOUS CHOICE

Here is a typical scenario that can have a major impact on your health. Suppose you are thirsty. Your first thought is to have a soda. But because you are aware of your choices and act, not just react, you choose a glass of water instead. You could even tell yourself that you'll have the soda after the water if you want. Chances are, the water will have satisfied your thirst and you won't even want the soda. With this one simple distinction, you have made a choice for health and saved a bit of money in the process. Imagine if you took that amount of money every day, or every time you thought about having a soda, and put it into an interest-bearing savings account. Over a period of years you could actually accumulate a small fortune by that one simple action.

These simple daily choices will, over time, help you to have a happier, healthier, more fulfilling life.

COMMITMENT

The one characteristic that separates successful people from the rest of the pack is that successful people are totally committed to their dreams and goals. Successful people don't give up at the first sign of difficulty—they persevere. Successful people don't give in to laziness and procrastination; they have developed a level of commitment that is stronger than the urge to slack off.

How many people do you know who went into a business with all the excitement of a small child on Christmas morning only to quit at the first hurdle? Perhaps you've done this. I know I have. There have been times when I have ventured into a business only to give up at the first challenge because I had not developed a total commitment to make it work.

JUST DO IT

Several years ago I was considering joining a health club, but when I thought about the upcoming winter I knew I wouldn't want to make the trip several times a week. I had no commitment. Last year, however, I had become tired of not looking and feeling my best. I once again investigated the health club possibility. I had to do something. This time I joined. I set goals and developed a strong commitment to follow through. As mentioned previously, I knew I had the necessary commitment when one morning at 6 A.M. with the outside temperature below zero, I found myself putting on my workout clothes and going to the club.

What had changed? All the conditions were the same as before. The only thing that had changed was me. I had developed a strong enough commitment that no matter what, regardless of the weather or any other circumstance, I was going to follow my program. I'm succeeding in attaining better health and becoming more fit because I'm committed.

The following quote from German philosopher Goethe demonstrates the power of commitment.

Until one is committed,
there is hesitancy,
the chance to draw back,
always ineffectiveness.
Concerning all acts of initiative
there is one elementary truth,
the ignorance of which kills
countless ideas and endless plans:
That the moment one definitely commits oneself,
then providence moves, too.
All sorts of things occur to help one
that would never otherwise have occurred.
A whole stream of events issues from the decision,
raising in one's favor all manner of
unforeseen incidents and meetings and
material assistance which no man

could have dreamed would come his way.
Whatever you can do or dream you can, begin it!
Boldness has genius, power, and magic in it.

WHAT ABOUT YOU?

At some point you have to be willing to "put it on the line." There is an old saying that if you don't stand for something, you'll fall for anything. What do you stand for? Do you have the integrity to hold to your values and commitment no matter what? I believe you do. Whatever your dreams and goals, it's your level of commitment that will make them a reality.

Are you willing to continue your effort and not quit? If you have your own business or are planning to start one, will you risk possible rejection, setbacks, and yes, even failure, to pursue your dream? Will you put it all on the line and refuse to give up, no matter the odds? If you can honestly answer yes to this question, you will greatly increase your chance for success. I would even go so far as to say that all else being equal, the person with the strongest commitment will succeed when all others fail. As the Goethe quote states, "Once you are committed, even providence moves too."

JIMMY, THE PRINTER

My friend Jimmy left his job to start his own business. When he began, I had asked him how he felt about his new challenge. "I'll give it six months," he replied, "and if it doesn't work, I'll get another job." As you may have already guessed, he went out of business in about four months. Fortunately, the story has a happy ending. He and his wife have started a new venture. They have a new printing business. This time their children are playing in the waiting room and Jimmy's wife, Ann, is doing the typesetting.

When I asked him how he felt about the new venture, he said "Great!" He told me they had everything on the line and were going to make it succeed. The last time I visited, they had several employees, had expanded into larger quarters and were running two shifts. Clearly their level of commitment to the second business enabled them to build a successful enterprise and create the life they want.

When things don't go the way you want, it's your level of commitment that is tested. If your commitment is strong, you will get through whatever is happening. Whether you're in a new relationship, starting a business, or want to lose a few pounds, the same principle applies. You must be totally committed if you want to succeed.

BURNING BRIDGES

Suppose for a moment you want to start your own business. It's a good way to give yourself some protection against being downsized. Today, many people are facing the challenges and reaping the rewards of self-employment.

If you're starting a new business, you must get committed to success. In his classic book, *Think and Grow Rich,* Napoleon Hill talks about "burning all your bridges." The reason he suggests burning your bridges is that if you have no other choice, you will use all of your resources to accomplish what you want. Be careful of the trap of fence sitting. This practice has been the downfall of many well-intentioned people. You must be committed. Remember my friend Jimmy? When he finally got serious, he succeeded.

Of course, if you can build your business while keeping the security of a regular job and paycheck, by all means do it. There is no point in taking extra risk if you don't have to. Often the husband or wife will keep his or her job while the other spouse begins the business. This takes some of the pressure off and allows time for the young business to grow and flourish.

INCREASING YOUR COMMITMENT

How can you raise your level of commitment? How will you motivate yourself to take action, even in the face of adversity? What will get you out of bed and exercising on a frigid winter morning instead of pulling the blanket over your head and rolling over? What will drive you to make another sales call even if the last three people turned you down? How will you convince yourself to spend that all-important time with your family when your friends are all going golfing? Leverage.

Your answer will be determined by the amount of leverage you can use to maintain and support your commitment. Let's face it, everything we do is either to gain pleasure or to avoid pain. To develop a strong, powerful, and steadfast commitment, we need to gain leverage on ourselves.

Other people are already using this simple concept to motivate us. Your boss does it by saying something like, "Fred, if you reach the sales quota by January, you'll receive a four percent bonus." You weigh the benefit (pleasure) versus the effect (pain) and decide what you will do. If the pleasure to be gained outweighs the pain or perceived pain, you will do it. If the motivating factor (reward) is big enough, you can accomplish any goal.

If I were to ask you to walk 25 miles at night in the pouring rain and offer you $100 as a prize, you will probably not even consider it. However, if I change the reward and I offer you $100,000 cash to do it, chances are you'll be moving before I finish the sentence.

In the highly competitive field of professional selling, the top performers and achievers are rewarded with luxurious prizes for their efforts. This is sometimes a better motivator than even more money.

There are, however, some people who are more motivated by the fear of loss (or pain) than the promise of a reward. The principle still holds true.

Children react the same way. If you offer your teens a choice between mowing the lawn and having dessert, or not mowing the lawn and foregoing the dessert you will probably have really tall grass. If on the other hand, you change the outcome for not doing it to being grounded for a week, they will most likely cut the grass. An offer to use the family car for the night might be an even better motivator. Most people respond better to positive motivation.

Commitment Exercise

How do you make use of this principle of leverage to strengthen your commitment? It's really quite simple. In your journal, write a paragraph or two emphasizing all the benefits you will realize by staying committed and reaching your goal. Really pour it on. Remember, we want to link a lot of pleasure to staying committed. For your business goal, your benefit might be all the things you can buy for yourself and your family with the extra money. List them. It might be the faraway places you can visit and the pleasure you'll experience there. Perhaps it's the extra time you can spend with your loved ones or simply the sense of freedom knowing that you're in charge of your own destiny. Whatever it is for you, write it out.

Agony of Defeat

Next, on a new page, write all the pain you will experience if you don't follow through. What will you lose out on? What are you already losing out on by not having reached this goal? What will be the outcome if you don't follow through with your commitments? Maybe it will mean staying stuck in a job you dislike, working for a boss you don't respect, and doing it each and every day for the next 20 years or longer.

Future Pace

If you want to gain more commitment to a health goal, ask yourself, *What will I look and feel like in ten, twenty, or thirty years if I don't take this action now?* When I did that and saw clearly what my physical condition would be in thirty years if I didn't begin exercising now, it moved me so much

I put on a pair of sneakers and went out the door before I even completed the written exercise. That was several years ago, and I have maintained a pretty regular exercise program ever since. When I find myself slipping back into my old, lazy habits (and we all slip once in a while), I only need to repeat this exercise and the motivation and commitment returns. In anything, especially health and exercise, staying focused on a result will help you through the rough spots. Remind yourself why you're doing what you're doing.

World Class

Do you think Olympic gold medal winners just love to practice? Of course not. I'm sure they would rather do other things during the hundreds of days of practice leading up to an Olympic event, but they stay centered because their focus is on the medal. They see themselves in the winner's circle and see and feel the roar of the crowd. That's what keeps them going through all the hard work it takes to be a world-class athlete.

You are a world-class person, too. Stay focused on your result. Use the leverage exercise to help you stay committed to your life and I assure you that you will live a life beyond your wildest imaginations.

Chapter 8

Action

Once you've gone through the process of identifying what you want to change in your life, developed new empowering beliefs, made a real commitment to change your life, identified your dreams, became excited about the possibilities that lie ahead, broken through your fears, strengthened your faith, and set your goals, the next and most crucial step is *action*.

You must be willing to do your part. You must be willing to do the "legwork." Your part is to take action—massive action. If you want a big life, take big action.

FOCUS ON RESULTS

It's important for you to keep your part in perspective. Your job is to define and set your goals and take appropriate action toward them. Stay focused on your desired result. You may self-sabotage by trying to control the "how" of getting what you want.

A good example of trying to control the how is the story of Linda, a woman in one of my workshops. The first night of the workshop she shared that one of her goals was to go on a vacation. She wrote it down and set a goal to do it. The following week, she shared that her sister was taking her on an all-expense paid trip to Hawaii. When I asked her why she was not excited that her goal came to be in such a short time, she exclaimed that this didn't count because her goal was to pay for it herself. I suggested that she accept the gift graciously and realize she had reached her goal of going on a cruise. The details of how were not her responsibility.

Once when I was rebuilding my life after having been at a very low point, I didn't have a car. It wasn't a major problem because I was able to use public transportation, but one of my immediate goals was to obtain a car. I had set it as a goal and went about my business. One night I was having dinner with my sister Debbie and her boyfriend, when out of the blue he said to me, "By the way, I know you need a car, and I happen to have one in a garage. It's not great to look at but it runs well, and it's yours for as long as you need it." Did I say, "No, I want to buy my own?" You bet I didn't. I said, "Thank you" and graciously accepted his generous offer.

STAY OPEN TO OPPORTUNITY

Our job is to know what we want and to take action toward obtaining it. The details of how and when are not always in our hands. In time, we will have everything we ask for. It's important to remain open to all possibilities and all avenues. If your goal is to increase your wealth and you find a dime on the street, pick it up and give thanks for the increase. Affirm that your wealth is increasing. Don't turn your back on opportunity just because you think you know how life should unfold. You aren't the Creator of the universe. Simply do your part, and everything will work out for your highest good.

TAKE AN IMMEDIATE FIRST STEP

One of the most important components of the action principle is to take an immediate first step. By this I mean that once you have decided upon your goals, look at each one and ask yourself what you can do right now, today, this minute, to begin moving in the direction of reaching these goal. What small, simple action can you take that will start you on your desired path?

For example, if your goal is to get in better physical shape and be healthier, a simple first action could be to just put on a pair of sneakers and go for a walk. Another might be to make an appointment to tour a health club.

If one of your goals is to improve your marriage, you could call a florist and send your wife flowers for no particular reason, other than you love her. Or you could stop by a travel agency and pick up a brochure for a romantic getaway that your husband has been hinting about.

If one of your goals is to start your own business, you might begin by going to a business opportunity meeting. You could buy and read a book or two about starting a business. There are dozens of great books about becoming an entrepreneur.

Action Exercise

In your journal or goals workbook, make a list of each of your important one-year or short-term goals. Next to each, write one simple action step you will take right away. Then, go and do it.

Action is Power

Taking action is a very powerful step for several reasons. First, it signals your subconscious mind that you're serious about this goal. It delivers the message that you're going for it and removes any doubt as to whether this is a real goal or just an empty wish. Next, it brings into play the law of physics that states that a force in motion tends to stay in motion until acted upon by a greater or more powerful outside force. Once you have begun moving on your path, it's likely you will continue. So begin now. An added benefit is the immediate gratification that comes from taking action on your goals. You'll begin to feel a sense of certainty about what you're doing, and this will help motivate you further.

Massive Action

It's true that if you want a big life, you need big dreams. It's also true that if you want big results you need to take massive action. Once when I was trying to lose weight but not getting results, I went to a friend who had successfully lost a lot of weight. When I told him that I had been walking for 20 minutes three times a week but not losing weight, he said to me, "How many days are there in a week?" Of course I replied, "Seven." "Then, walk seven days and you'll lose weight." I did, and it worked. If you're taking action and not getting the results you're looking for, either you're taking incorrect action or you're not taking enough action.

Massive action will produce massive change. Assuming your actions are in the right direction and you are getting a result, you can increase the level of your results by taking more action. Simple, isn't it?

INCREASING THE ODDS

For example, if you are making ten telephone calls each day to prospective customers for your business and succeeding with one or two in getting the appointments that you want, then by making 50 or even 100 calls, you will be five to ten times more successful and produce a 500-1000 percent increase in your business.

Actually, your results will be even better because your massive action will have made you even more proficient in your technique, and your percentage of successful calls will have increased.

If, as in my fitness example, you want to get in better physical shape and are walking 20 minutes, three days a week (this amount, by the way, will enable you to maintain your present level of fitness), try increasing this to 30 minutes five or six times a week. You'll more than double your results.

HAVE A PLAN

Simply taking a lot of action, however, will get you nothing but tired and frustrated, unless you have a plan.

In your journal, write each of your major one-year goals on a separate page. Next, write out your action plan. Who will you talk with? What steps will you take? What milestones will you reach along the way? How will you measure your results?

For example, if you're working on a goal to increase your business, list the people you'll be working with. Brainstorm a list of prospects to call. Set "mini goals" along the way. Perhaps a "mini goal" would be reaching a specific income level from your personal efforts, at which point you will be able to afford additional marketing, like an Internet site, using some of the extra income you earned.

PLANNING YOUR WORK

I strongly suggest that you use some kind of daily or weekly planner, digital or otherwise. They have pages for monthly, weekly, and daily planning and appointments as well as to-do lists, address pages, notes, and other forms to help you become better organized. Use whatever size fits your lifestyle and work habits. I have tried them all and finally settled on an electronic device as best for me.

It has always amazed me how many small business people and entrepreneurs don't use a planner. I cannot imagine running my business life without one. Perhaps that's why so many people complain about being too busy and not accomplishing what they want to accomplish.

WEEKLY PLANNING

Using your short-term and one-year goals as a guide, you can set weekly "mini goals"—actions you will take that over time will move you toward your goals. Personally, I like to take at least a couple of actions each week toward my one-year and long-term goals.

SUCCESS TIP

When you are considering an activity, ask yourself, *Will what I'm planning to do bring me closer to or further away from my major goals?* This is a big help in deciding where to invest your time. If you're choosing between watching television and going to a business meeting, this question will help you remember what's most important for your future.

In addition to your goal-oriented actions, your weekly plan can include all of the other things you want to do that week. You might include exercise days, social engagements, meetings, chores, errands, important calls, etc. By using a weekly overview, it's easier to see where in your daily planner these activities can be scheduled.

PRIORITIES AND TIME MANAGEMENT

Too many people waste their precious time on what I call "busy work." We have all been guilty of this at one time or another. To avoid unpleasant tasks, we distract ourselves by "majoring in minors." Rather than risk possible rejection and the associated pain, we decide to take some time to get better organized. After all, we rationalize, a person needs to be well organized to succeed. So off we go to our local office supply store. We carefully shop for colored file folders, labels, business cards and letterhead paper, pens, new software (you'll need a good database) and an endless supply of other "essentials." This can be a death rattle as my friend Burke Hedges always says, "Don't confuse activity with productivity!"

Plan your work; work your plan. It has been proven that a one-hour investment in planning can save you ten hours of work. That's a 1,000 percent return on the time invested. If you interview highly successful people and high achievers, you'll learn that they tend to be well organized. They plan their work and work their plan. If you want to be more successful, learn to plan your activities before you act.

Learn to delegate. Let's face it, no one is great at everything. There will always be tasks and activities in which you excel and there will always be those that are difficult for you. Often the things we dislike or try to postpone are those things we don't do well. To really become and remain successful, you must learn to share the responsibility and rewards of your labor. Learn to delegate.

Do what you do best. Dr. Robert Schuller made a brilliant statement that I have integrated into my life. When asked how he was able to accomplish such great feats, he said, "I do only those activities that only I can do." What a concept! In other words, if someone else could just as easily do a task, he would delegate it. This freed his time to do those things that required his personal attention.

In other words, if you do that which only you can do and find others to assist you with the rest, you will accomplish more than if you try, as my wife is fond of saying, "to play all the instruments in the band."

This was one lesson I had to learn the hard way and it cost me a great deal, both emotionally and financially. I had been publishing a bimonthly newspaper for small businesses near where I live. It was designed to communicate information that would help businesses grow and prosper. While the idea was sound and the publication well received for its content, it didn't succeed. I made the (costly) mistake of attempting to do it all myself. I was the editor and publisher, salesperson, designer, bookkeeper, and did pretty much everything else except take it to the post office. It became an all-consuming task that took its toll on my health and my life. The day my wife, Georgia, commented that it was "aging me," I ceased publication. She had found the magic word (aging) that would shake me back into reality.

LET SETBACKS BE YOUR TEACHER

I have learned from my mistakes and now publish a new quarterly newsletter for home-based businesses. This time I have taken Dr. Schuller's advice and included other people. My partner, Julie Parker, loves to sell advertising, a task I would rather postpone. We have others handling various aspects of the publication. Because of my willingness to share the responsibility, this publication is succeeding, and I'm enjoying it more because I get to do what I love doing—writing, editing, and working with writers.

Do what you are good at. If you would rather be out selling than accounting, that's fine. Hire a bookkeeper. Surround yourself with a team of capable people and let them do what they do best.

Remember the brilliant statement from Zig Ziglar, "The way to get what you want in life is to help enough other people get what they want."

ONGOING PERSONAL DEVELOPMENT

Can you really increase your income by simply reading self-help books and listening to tapes, or is it just a bunch of hype designed by the people who write and record those books and tapes? Do these principles really work, or is it just a lot of "feel good, touchy feely" rubbish? Well, my friend, I can honestly tell you—yes, you can increase your income, and yes, the principles do work! In a moment, I will explain how and why.

Napoleon Hill in *Think and Grow Rich,* James Allen in *As a Man Thinketh,* and Florence Scovel Shinn in *The Game of Life*—all written in the 1900s—taught us we could use the power of our minds to become more successful.

Most people, especially if they have been in business for a while, have probably been to a seminar on personal development. Seminars are great. I love going to them, and I really love giving them because I can share ideas with a live audience and meet new people, something I really enjoy doing. The problem is, as I'm sure you've experienced, that a week or two after the seminar you are right back into your unproductive habits. You left the seminar all charged up, but after the excitement wore off, you slipped back into your pre-seminar behavior. Reading books and listening to self-help tapes is also a great practice but, like seminars, if not done on a regular basis the results are not nearly as powerful.

INVEST IN YOURSELF

The key is On-going Personal Development (OPD). The Japanese have a word, *kaizen,* which means making small daily improvements in every area of your life. It's a principle taught to them by the late W. Edwards Deming who went to Japan to help them rebuild after World War II. Since we have no word for this in English, I have chosen OPD as a reminder to follow this formula for success.

It's not so much what you do sometimes that makes the difference, it's what you do daily. Just as this applies to health and fitness, it applies to success. If you want to succeed and grow, make a daily habit of reading and listening to self-help and inspirational books and tapes. As little as ten minutes each morning can make a major difference. For one thing, you will begin your day on a more positive note; and second, you will over time have assimilated a lot of powerful, positive, and thought-provoking ideas.

PROOF POSITIVE

Several years ago my friend John came to visit me in my home office. It had been a while since I had seen him, so of course I asked how he had been. "Great!" he replied, "My income went up more than 15 percent in the past six months." Considering that John is in automobile sales and we were in the middle of the worst recession in decades, I had to learn more. I asked John how he did it and was a bit taken aback when he replied, "I went to a seminar." He went on to explain that the seminar leader suggested reading a self-help book for 15 to 30 minutes a day.

John, who had not read a book since graduation, bought the speaker's book and began reading every morning before going into the dealership where he worked. He would leave for work a half an hour early each day, sit outside in his car and read the book. That was the only change he made in his daily habits and his income increased by 15 percent, which, in John's case, worked out to be $100 an hour for reading! Would you read 30 minutes a day for $50?

It took me a long time to fully understand what had taken place, but it finally "clicked" one day. Imagine John, having just finished his daily ritual of reading an inspirational book, going into the showroom. He is in a positive, uplifted state and is probably cheerful and bouncy. The other salespeople are in the corner, kicking and grumping about the recession. You've seen the scene, everyone stands around complaining about the situation instead of taking action to change it.

You, the new car buyer, enter the showroom. On one side is the group kicking the coffee pot and looking grumpy. Across the room is John, bouncing around happy as can be. Now let me ask you the critical questions: From whom do you want to buy your car? Who are you most likely to gravitate toward? John, of course. Positive energy attracts people to it.

As a direct result of investing a little time each day on personal development (OPD), John increased his income and felt better in the process. The bonus is that this activity is cumulative. The more you do it, the better you feel.

SUCCESS LEAVES CLUES

One hundred percent of the self-made millionaires (excluding people in the entertainment field) are committed to reading and listening to self-help books and tapes. I personally credit the success I've enjoyed to my constant diet of positive, inspirational books, tapes, and seminars. My car is never without a tape or two, and I'm always reading a few books.

How many books have you read this month? How many tapes are in your car? Do you think it's a coincidence that companies like Gillette, Amway, McDonald's, Delta Airlines, IBM, AT&T, Century 21, General Motors, Marriott, Ford, and many others have formal employee development programs, using books and tapes, to encourage success in their workforce? All you need to do is look at the sales figures for these companies to see the results of these programs.

Chapter 9

Success Tools

*There is no surer way along the road to success than
to follow in the footsteps of those who have reached it.*
–Anonymous

In the following pages are some of the "tools" that I and many
others use to stay on track and condition our minds for a
happy and productive life. Use the ones that appeal to you
and leave the rest. Play with these and the other examples
from this book. Make it fun. Lighten up and enjoy yourself.

MIRROR WORK

Mirror work is powerful. It puts you face to face with yourself and can even be a bit unnerving at first. Stick with it and
you will be pleased with the results. Read and recite your affirmations into a mirror while looking deep into your own eyes.

VISUALIZATION

Sitting quietly and picturing what you want in your life
is another powerful tool. Perhaps the most powerful, because

it involves more of your senses. While there are several good books written about visualization, it's fairly simple to begin.

BE STILL

Sit quietly in a comfortable place where you won't be disturbed. Relax. Take several deep breaths and become quiet. When you feel relaxed, simply close your eyes and picture a screen. On this screen, you will project a picture of what you want. Imagine what you want in as much detail as you can. Don't force this, just stay relaxed and see it happen. Use color, sound, smells, and draw upon all of your senses. If, for example, you're picturing your own home, see all of the details of that house. You can put yourself in the picture. See your family there as well. Make it as vivid and bright as you can. Don't strain, simply relax and see the picture.

Invest time in this tool on a daily basis and you will be amazed at how much it speeds the time it takes to actually reach your goals. You need not spend a long time. Five or ten minutes is fine. What you're doing is communicating to your subconscious mind a clear picture of what you want. You need to continue to do the legwork, but don't obsess about how this will happen. It just will.

TREASURE MAPS

Treasure maps are powerful tools that use your visual senses to keep you on track. A treasure map is simply a collection of pictures that represent what you want to have in your life. It can be a simple picture of a new car, or it can be a complex collage that represents your ideal life.

You can include pictures of things you want, places you want to visit, and feelings you want to experience. Treasure maps can really be fun. You can draw them, cut pictures from magazines, use photos, or whatever else you can think of to represent your goals. Place your treasure map where you will see it regularly. Mine, which grew from a simple 11" x 14" framed collage to a full 24" x 36" wall hanging, is in my home office where I see it daily. This is simply another way to stay focused and keep your mind on what matters to you most. You are imprinting your goals on your subconscious mind.

KEEP A JOURNAL

One of my mentors, Tony Robbins, once said that, "A life worth living is a life worth recording." Keep a journal of your thoughts, ideas, progress, and everything you are experiencing in your life. I have several years worth of journals, and it's great to go back and read what my dreams were, say, six or seven years ago. It's great reinforcement when I realize how many of my goals have been reached. A journal is a wonderful way to record your life. Some people write in their journals every day. Personally, like most things in my life, I do it in moderation.

Your journal is where you will record your dreams and goals, an activity that you will want to do at least twice a year. I usually reevaluate and do a goal-setting exercise at the beginning of the year and on my birthday, which just happens to be in June, six months into the year. By all means, invest time on your birthday thinking about your life, your dreams, and your goals. This is one of your most powerful days. A day when all the planetary forces are in your favor.

MANIFESTATION FILE

A practice I've begun recently is keeping a file of the things from my treasure map, which I have already received. One day I was removing some pictures from my treasure map because I had already received the items, and rather than throw them away, I put them into a file. At one of my workshops, someone suggested labeling it my "manifestation file" and keeping the pictures of goals that are now part of my life. This serves to remind me of just how many of my goals and dreams have come to pass.

GRATITUDE LIST

One of the ways to remain in a positive state of mind is to develop an attitude of gratitude about your life. Whatever your present condition, there are things for which you can be grateful. What about your physical and mental health? Your family and friends? Look around where you live. Consider your possessions, your job. For all of those things you tend to take for granted, you can be grateful.

Gratitude is one of the major keys to happiness. If you're feeling grateful for what you have, you'll be a happy person.

On the other hand, if you're constantly focusing on what you don't have, you will be miserable most of the time. Remember that what you think about expands. If you spend your time thinking about how lucky you are and how grateful you feel, then that will expand as well.

Write down all the things in your life you are grateful for, and when you're feeling down, take out your list and read it. When you feel grateful, add that to the list. If you can't find anything to be grateful about, visit people in a hospital or homeless shelter and compare your problems with theirs.

PEOPLE TO MEET

Keep a list of the people you would most like to meet. As in goal-setting, simply writing down the names increases greatly the chance of it happening.

IDEAS LIST

We have ideas pop into our minds all the time. The problem is that most of us either forget about our ideas, discard them because we think they are of no value, or are too wild, or we just never act on our ideas. By keeping an ideas list, we eliminate the chance of forgetting what may be a major idea. Some of the most successful businesses in the world were built on the simplest of ideas.

Do you know the story of the ice cream vendor at the 1934 World's Fair who, when he ran out of paper cups for his ice cream, borrowed some of those flat, Belgian waffles from the vendor down the way (who was not selling many anyway), and created what has become accepted worldwide as the ice cream cone? Keep your mind open to new combinations and new possibilities.

YOUR DEFINITE MAJOR PURPOSE

If you had all the money you needed and couldn't fail, what would do? What are you here on earth to accomplish? How can you best invest your time and energy? What is the unique contribution that only you can make to the world? What is important to you? In your journal, write your definite major purpose in as much detail as you can. We are all here to do something. If you are one of those fortunate enough to uncover what that is and willing to go ahead and do it, you will lead a life beyond your wildest dreams.

A PROMISE TO YOURSELF

Congratulations! By finishing this book, you have just taken a major step forward in creating the life you deserve to live. If you skipped over any of the exercises, please go back and do them now. These are some important "tools" you can use as you progress in your journey toward success.

Decide now to live your dreams. You have the necessary tools. You have identified what you want in your life.

Now, it's up to you.

Promise yourself and your family that you will pursue these dreams to the best of your ability.

Decide now that you will succeed.

Decide now that you will let nothing stop you!

You, and only you, can decide to act. Whatever you want in life, it's there waiting for you. All you need to do is decide what you want, take action, and in the words of Sir Winston Churchill, "Never, never, never, never give up."

And may I add: "Always, always, always live your dreams!"

Conclusion

There you have it. Time-tested, proven ideas and techniques you can use to create a life that is beyond your wildest imagination. I know. I've done it. It's now up to you.

Are you willing to do the legwork? Are you willing to let go of your old limiting beliefs, change your destructive habits, decide what you really want, put those desires in writing, set goals, and have the kind of life that you want and deserve?

And finally, are you willing to take the necessary action to accomplish this and create the life that you want? By now you are well on your way to "designing" the life of your dreams.

Write in your journal regularly to track your progress and record your life. You really can have the life of your dreams. Remember to do it now—what are you waiting for? It's your life!

Be well,
Jim

Acknowledgments

This book is dedicated to God and the Angels who have watched over and protected me and are the inspiration for everything I write.

To Georgia, my wife and best friend for her belief in my work, endless patience and support of my mission.

To my sister Debbie Donovan for being there for me when I hit bottom and needed help.

My longtime friend and Mastermind partner Art (Ski) Swiatkowski for helping me stay on track and accountable but, most of all, for being my friend in living the dream.

To Michelle Colon Johnson for introducing me to Sound Wisdom.

To Dave Wildasin, General Manager at Sound Wisdom, for his support of this book and interest in publishing it.

To Terri Meckes, Christina Lynch, and Lisa Ott, my awesome production team at Sound Wisdom.

Special thanks to Beth Meininger for sharing her insights and ideas.

To Catherine Colletta for her assistance in the preparation of this book.

Of course my endless gratitude to all of the great minds who have shared their ideas and experiences so that we all may grow and prosper.

Most of all, I want to thank the many readers of *What Are You Waiting For?* and my *Jim's Jems* newsletter who took the time to write and share their successes with me. It's their dedication to creating a better life that motivates me to be the best I can be. As my friend, Terri Lonier, once said, "We're all in this together."

About Jim Donovan

Jim Donovan, a native New Yorker, has implemented the timeless principles in his books to first turn his own life around and then devote his life to helping others do the same. Jim practices these principles every day and is living proof that they work.

A best-selling author whose books are published in 22 countries and a highly sought-after motivational speaker, he has touched the lives of hundreds of thousands of people who want a better life. Crossing all ethnic, age, and gender barriers, his simple message has been embraced by teenagers and executives alike. From business leaders to single parents, people around the world are improving the quality of their lives by following the simple techniques in his books and programs.

After living through personal challenges for a decade and a downward spiral that left him homeless, friendless, and penniless, Jim reached out for help. Wanting to have a better life, he became a student of self-help literature; and seeing the results in his own life, he began writing his "Jim's

Jems" newsletter and delivering seminars to help others. This led to his first book and a life dedicated to helping people tap into the power within them and create the life they were born to live.

Jim's practical techniques and powerful stories have made him a life-changing speaker for businesses, trade groups, and associations. His seminars have benefited audiences nation-wide, including banks, medical practices, accounting firms, small business groups, chambers of commerce, women-owned businesses, associations, government, network marketing companies, school faculties and students. He also delivers his Yes You Can seminar as a volunteer in adult and youth correctional facilities.

Jim's seminars inspire audiences to take responsibility for their lives, provide them with transformational ideas and strategies for their success, and motivate them to take charge of their destiny and create the life they were born to live.

Visit www.jimdonovan.com to sign up for a free subscription to *Jim's Jems* e-zine for personal and professional growth. Published since 1992, it is read by individuals and business people worldwide. The author can also be reached by writing: Jim Donovan, PO Box 63, Upper Black Eddy, PA 18972.

Journaling

_____

_____

_____

_____

_____

_____

_____

_____

_____

_____

_____

_____

_____

_____

_____

Journaling

_____

_____

_____

_____

_____

_____

_____

_____

_____

_____

_____

_____

_____

_____

_____

Journaling

_____

_____

_____

_____

_____

_____

_____

_____

_____

_____

_____

_____

_____

_____

_____

_____

Journaling

Journaling

_____

_____

_____

_____

_____

_____

_____

_____

_____

_____

_____

_____

_____

_____

_____

_____

Journaling

_____

_____

_____

_____

_____

_____

_____

_____

_____

_____

_____

_____

_____

_____

_____

Journaling

_____

_____

_____

_____

_____

_____

_____

_____

_____

_____

_____

_____

_____

_____

_____

_____

Journaling

_____

_____

_____

_____

_____

_____

_____

_____

_____

_____

_____

_____

_____

_____

_____

_____

Journaling

_____

_____

_____

_____

_____

_____

_____

_____

_____

_____

_____

_____

_____

_____

_____

_____

Journaling

_____

_____

_____

_____

_____

_____

_____

_____

_____

_____

_____

_____

_____

_____

Journaling

_____

_____

_____

_____

_____

_____

_____

_____

_____

_____

_____

_____

_____

_____

_____

_____

Journaling

Journaling

_____

_____

_____

_____

_____

_____

_____

_____

_____

_____

_____

_____

_____

_____

_____

_____

Journaling

_____

_____

_____

_____

_____

_____

_____

_____

_____

_____

_____

_____

_____

_____

_____

_____